Spectacular Atonement

Langham
GLOBAL LIBRARY

If there is any biblical or theological concept that needs all the attention that we can give it in Africa, it is Christ's atoning death. I grew up watching my parents and our neighbours pouring out libations and offering animal sacrifices to appease the gods or the spirits of our ancestors. Those practices were assumed to take our place and prevent us from facing their wrath. On the one hand, coming from that experiential worldview helps African Christians appreciate the atonement. On the other hand, coming out of such a primordial worldview into the Christian faith and practice may make it difficult for African Christians to have a clear grasp of the atonement.

African theologians need to carefully tease out certain biblical concepts, including the concept of atonement. Doing this will help African Christianity to avoid the temptation of eclipsing or distorting the biblical interpretation of the atonement. Dr. Robert Falconer's book, *Spectacular Atonement: Envisioning the Cross of Christ in an African Perspective,* has made a significant contribution to our understanding of this key area of theology in Africa. He has provided an important resource for African Christian theologians, theological educators, students of theology and Christian mission workers to help African Christians be deeply rooted in the faith. This is a must-read book! I recommend it to Christians, Christian professionals and theological educators both in private and public institutions across Africa.

Sunday Bobai Agang, PhD
Provost,
ECWA Theological Seminary, Jos (JETS), Nigeria

Christianity is an alive and growing religion in many African contexts. This presents both promise and peril for the faith and persons entering the Christian faith across the continent. This book presents an appreciative and a critical engagement with some important theories of atonement in relation to African contexts, cultures and philosophies. I highly recommend it to African Christian theologians and those who have an interest in the decolonization and contextualization of African Christianity.

Dion A. Forster, PhD
Chair of Systematic Theology and Ecclesiology,
University of Stellenbosch, South Africa

I could not agree with Dr. Falconer more: "For Christians, the cross of Christ is perhaps the most dramatic and spectacular event in history." However, the message of the cross does not ring loudly in many African pulpits or theological discussions. Pulpits in many churches in Africa preach a self-centred message of perpetual prosperity, often one that is severed from the centrality of the cross of Christ and its cosmic ramifications. Many theologians see the motif of penal substitution within the atonement as a guilt-oriented concept, more useful perhaps for Christians in the global north. They argue that the African context benefits more from the Christus Victor motif, given the realities of the spirit world. Dr. Falconer does the church of Jesus Christ in Africa a great service of bridging these two atonement motifs by critically examining their historical development and paying close attention to the biblical texts to engage with Christian life and theology within the African cultural context.

This book will be a helpful text for systematic theology and even for pastoral ministry classes. This book shows how the church's practices of discipleship, preaching and apologetics can be enriched through helpful contextual theology that is grounded in the Scriptures but always looking outwards to the perennial African issues such as ancestors, evil spirits, suffering and witchcraft, thereby "offering liberty and hope." I highly recommend this book as biblically faithful, theologically astute, African-oriented and ministerially focused.

Kevin Muriithi Ndereba, PhD
Lecturer and Head of Department,
Department of Practical Theology, St. Paul's University, Kenya

In this work, the author offers a harmonized clear perspective of Christus Victor and penal substitution demonstrating that Christ is all-sufficient to fulfil the African Christian holistic yearning for him. Here lies the necessary foundational truth for every follower or seeker of Christ. The book lays a very helpful etic basis in bringing Christ to the centre of African cultural transformation. This book is a treasure for every Christian. Whether you are a student of the word, a pastor or a theologian, this book is a great resource for teaching, reflection and ministry.

David Ngaruiya, PhD
Associate Professor,
International Leadership University, Kenya

Spectacular Atonement is a well-argued book that puts into dialogue the various strands of historic Christian interpretations of the atonement, together with African interpretations and understandings of the atoning work of Christ. It is theologically, biblically and culturally grounded and is practical in applying the efficacy of Christ's victory on the cross. This book is a valuable addition to the quest for an authentic African Christian theology.

James Nkansah-Obrempong, PhD
Professor of Theology and Dean, School of Theology-NEGST,
Africa International University, Kenya

In *Spectacular Atonement: Envisioning the Cross of Christ in an African Perspective* Dr. Robert Falconer argues that atonement includes both penal substitution and the Christ as Victor motif, both in the Scriptures, and from an African perspective. Falconer shows this harmony by considering historical theology through the lenses of African theologians. He follows the footsteps of theologians before him as he engages with the key issues of articulating atonement theology for the African cultural and philosophical contexts.

Falconer's book is a must-have for theologians, students and other scholars. He elevates, as of uttermost importance, Christ, and his atoning work, over the African understanding of God, hence Jesus's spectacular atonement.

This book will be especially useful to those seeking to unravel how the yearnings of the African people in their traditions become fulfilled in the cross of Christ, which made them a new creation.

Rev. Canon Francis Omondi, PhD
Canon, All Saints Cathedral Kampala, Church of Uganda
Adjunct Lecturer, St. Paul's University, Kenya

Spectacular Atonement by Dr. Robert Falconer is fascinating, insightful, creative and innovative. The historical doctrine of atonement is made simple for African readers. The author draws new insights, interpretations and criticisms from the wealth of biblical scholarship and materials. The true meaning of atonement hangs on two complementary concepts: penal substitution and Christus Victor. This book focuses on the harmony between penal substitution and Christus Victor as defined in both Scripture and theological writings. Ultimately, the author makes the African perspective of atonement deliberate, instructive and methodological. Thus, atonement in both its meaning and application is couched and understood from African thought and worldview as distinct from western thought patterns and concepts.

Yusufu Turaki, PhD
Professor of Theology and Social Ethics,
ECWA Theological Seminary, Jos (JETS), Nigeria

Throughout this captivating book, Dr. Robert Falconer eloquently justifies his use of "spectacular" in the title. The author grew up in Africa where he has spent his professional life as a theological educator. This background is demonstrated in his multifaceted Scriptural exposition of the closely related themes of substitutionary atonement (the cross) and its divine-human agent, the victorious Christ. Of special value is the author's perceptive application to crucial worldview issues and the challenges being faced in the contemporary African setting. I highly commend this insightful, accessible study as one that all Christians in Africa will learn and benefit from.

Ernst R. Wendland, PhD
Visiting Professor, Department of Ancient Studies,
University of Stellenbosch, South Africa

Spectacular Atonement

Envisioning the Cross of Christ in
an African Perspective

Robert Falconer

Langham

GLOBAL LIBRARY

© 2023 Robert Falconer

Published 2023 by Langham Global Library
An imprint of Langham Publishing
www.langhampublishing.org

Langham Publishing and its imprints are a ministry of Langham Partnership

Langham Partnership
PO Box 296, Carlisle, Cumbria, CA3 9WZ, UK
www.langham.org

ISBNs:
978-1-83973-736-7 Print
978-1-83973-817-3 ePub
978-1-83973-819-7 PDF

British Library Cataloguing-in-Publication Data
A catalogue record for this book is available from the British Library

ISBN: 978-1-83973-736-7

Cover & Book Design: projectluz.com

For my African sons, Ezekiel and Gabriel Falconer

Contents

Foreword xiii

Preface xv

1   Introduction 1

Part 1

2   Atonement in Scripture 7

3   Atonement in Christian Theology 29

4   Atonement in African Christianity 55

Part 2

5   African Spirituality 63

6   Atonement in African Traditional Ritual 69

7   The Problem of the African Idea of God 75

8   Christ and the Ancestors 81

9   The Cross of Christ and Evil Spirits 93

10 The Cross of Christ and Sin 99

11 The Cross of Christ and Witchcraft 105

12 The Cross of Christ and Suffering 113

13 A New African Humanity 121

14 Cosmic Harmony and an African Hope 131

Bibliography 141

Foreword

The major task of every good theology is primarily twofold. First, it is the duty of every good theology to articulate the meaning of a word or concept. Second, a good theology must apply that meaning to the contemporary situation or context. This book, *Spectacular Atonement: Envisioning the Cross of Christ in an African Perspective*, by Dr. Robert Falconer, seeks to meet these two basic requirements.

The book is divided into two parts.

Part 1 carefully examines the meaning of the atonement in Scripture, Christian theology and African Christianity. Here the author critically examines various theological positions on the meaning of the atonement, and concludes by giving a strong defence of the harmony of the penal substitutionary atonement and Christus Victor themes. This theological position provides the author the foundation and the basis from which he approaches the meaning of the atonement in the African context. Dr. Falconer therefore engages both African Christian scholars and African Christianity on how they have articulated the meaning of the atonement for the African cultural and religious context.

Part 2 examines the African worldview vis-à-vis the Western worldview, which is alien to African thought. For Africans, the physical and the spiritual are tightly interwoven. Dr. Falconer argues that the death of Christ on the cross must have practical significance in the lives of Africans. Though there are many useful concepts in the African worldview, there are some ideas that require transformation. Regarding the concept of God, the author argues that the cross of Christ is the primary factor that distinguishes the biblical God from the African concept of God. Concerning the role of ancestors, Dr. Falconer argues that Christ is the Supreme Ancestor and therefore makes redundant the functions of other ancestors. Applying the Christus Victor theme, which is prevalent in Scripture, the author argues that the atonement has completely overcome evil forces, witchcraft, suffering, sin and fear, of all forms of evil.

Also of great importance is the forceful argument that an understanding of the cross of Christ will restore the important, though diminishing, understanding of the African concept of community. It is only the penal substitutionary atonement and the Christus Victor theme that can provide an adequate explanation for the yearnings, hope and redemption of the African people.

There are many books on the meaning of the cross of Christ, which focus either on the spiritual aspect (sin, repentance, forgiveness, heaven and so on) or just on the here and now. Here, in this book, we have an excellent balance that needs to be heard in clear terms. Africans need to know that Christ's death brings not just freedom from eternal condemnation and a guarantee of eternal bliss, but that this death of Christ has given total victory over the forces of evil and economic, social and political bondage.

I enthusiastically recommend this book as an important resource for those preparing for ministry, pastors, teachers in theological institutions and all those seeking to understand the meaning of Christianity for Africans.

Samuel Waje Kunhiyop, PhD
Author of *African Christian Ethics* and *African Christian Theology*
Previously Executive General Secretary, Evangel Fellowship International,
and ECWA General Secretary

Preface

For Christians, the cross of Christ is perhaps the most dramatic and spectacular event in history. It has captured the minds and hearts of countless theologians. The words of the apostle Paul are a case in point: "For I decided to know nothing among you except Jesus Christ and him crucified" (1 Cor 2:2). These words have shaped much of my own thinking and theology. I remember reading every book on the atonement that I could lay my hands on, often importing books from overseas because I could not find them in my own country. I presented my ideas of Christ's atoning work to two professors, Samuel Kunhiyop and Frank Jabini, and they insisted that I consider looking at the atonement from an African perspective. I took up the challenge and began reading about Africa and African Christianity. It helped that I had lived in South Africa for most of my life and grew up as a child in the Transkei, previously a homeland for the Xhosa people, in what was then the Cape Province. And so Africa and its people were not too unfamiliar to me.

A major part of my doctoral research took me on a fascinating journey, where I studied the implications of the atonement in African metaphysics. Metaphysics is a branch of philosophy which seeks to understand the nature of being. Exploring the cross of Christ in an African perspective has led my life in an entirely different direction. Soon after my studies, I married Catherine – Lady Cath, as I like to call her. She has served as a missionary for many years all over Africa, including in Khayelitsha (a major slum in Cape Town, South Africa), Sierra Leone, South Sudan, as well as several other African countries. I left the architectural practice in South Africa where I worked, and began work in Kenya as a missionary, serving as the principal of our mission organization's Bible school, DIGUNA Discipleship Training (DDT). At the DDT we discipled and trained young Christians, as well as church leaders from all over Eastern Africa. Today, I serve as the Coordinator of Student Research at the South African Theological Seminary (SATS).

I am very grateful to both Professor Kunhiyop and Professor Jabini for their guidance. Cath and others have seen the need for such a book, and I am thankful for their encouragement and support. I also owe gratitude to Dr. Bill Domeris, who read the manuscript and offered valuable comments and suggestions. Michael Smith read the manuscript with a keen eye on grammar and spelling, and I am grateful for his services too.

This book has two parts. In part 1, I begin in chapter 2 by exploring the atonement in Scripture, without being exhaustive in exposition. I purpose to demonstrate the harmony of penal substitution and Christ as Victor in Scripture. In chapter 3, we will look at atonement in Christian theology. This chapter will again focus on this same harmony of penal substitution and Christus Victor, but in light of historical theology. Many theologians, as we will discover, have sought to engage with the overarching predicaments of their time, articulating an atonement theology that was meaningful for the cultural and philosophical contexts in which they lived. Lastly, in chapter 4 we will look at atonement in African Christianity. Africa also enjoys expressions of atonement theology influenced by the continent's cultural context. This chapter seeks to outline how African theologians and Christian leaders understand Christ's atonement.

Part 2 focuses on African concerns. The first chapter in part 2 (chapter 5) explores African spirituality and the African worldview. Here we will see that for Africans, the "physical" and the "spiritual" are tightly interwoven. This chapter provides the context in which to place further discussions of the cross of Christ in an African perspective. We then move on to atonement in African traditional rituals in chapter 6. This chapter demonstrates how traditional atoning sacrifices and rituals fulfil the spiritual and philosophical needs of Africans, and that indeed many forms of traditional sacrifices are important for Africans. I will argue that African Christianity should employ that which is useful and biblical from within its own African worldview to communicate the cross of Christ without compromising the gospel. Next, in chapter 7 I discuss the problem of the African idea of God. I position Christ and his atoning work in relation to the African understanding of God, and demonstrate that the cross of Christ is the primary factor that distinguishes the God of Scripture from the African idea of God. Of great importance is the next chapter, chapter 8 on Christ and the ancestors. This chapter places Jesus and his cross in the very centre of African ancestry. The implications of the superiority of Jesus Christ through his cross are spectacular. Then the next four chapters (chapters 9–12) address very real fears that are faced by many Africans. These are evil spirits, sin, witchcraft and suffering. After this, in chapter 13 I show how an understanding of the cross of Christ in an African perspective may well offer optimism and hope for a new African humanity. The last chapter, chapter 14 on cosmic harmony and an African hope, is the climax of this book. Here the implications of the cross of Christ are in fact intrinsically this-worldly and physical in light of the new creation, fulfilling the very yearnings of the African people as revealed in their myths and traditions.

Robert Falconer
St Francis Bay, South Africa

1

Introduction

The theology of the cross of Christ primarily involves atonement theology, and throughout this book I will discuss this theology in terms of penal substitution and the victorious Christ, sometimes called "Christus Victor." I believe that they are two sides of the same coin, and both play a significant part in atonement theology. At the outset, I wish to make clear what I mean by both penal substitution and Christus Victor.

In penal substitution, "penal" refers to punishment, coming from the word "penalty," and "substitution" is someone or something taking the place of another. Sometimes, for whatever reason, a person may take the punishment in the place of the guilty party, the one for whom the punishment was meant. In penal substitutionary atonement, Jesus suffers and dies on a cross, taking upon himself the sin of the world (1 Pet 2:24), the sin of each and every one of us, and suffers the punishment and wrath of God which was meant for us because of our sin and rebellion against God (Rom 3:10–26). Jesus stands in our place as if he were us, and suffers the consequences of our sin, so that we might never have to experience the eternal punishment that was meant for us (2 Cor 5:19–21).

The idea of penal substitution was, in one way or another, evident in the writings of the church fathers early in the church's history, and it continued to develop. But it was really only at the time of the Reformation, under Martin Luther and John Calvin, that penal substitution was actually articulated, finding greater expression. The doctrine argues that Christ, by his own sacrificial choice, was punished (penalized) in the place of sinners (substitution), thereby satisfying the demands of justice so that God could justly forgive our sins, and so the substitutionary nature of Jesus's death is understood in the sense of a substitutionary punishment.

The term "Christus Victor," on the other hand, refers to a Christian understanding of the atonement in which Christ's death is the means by which the powers of evil, which held humankind under their power, were defeated. It is a view of the atonement that is also dated to the church fathers.

The Christus Victor theme is not as rational and systematic as is penal substitutionary atonement: rather, it is understood as a drama in the grand narrative of Scripture, whereby God through his Son triumphed over Satan and the evil spirits and defeated them, liberating humanity from the bondage of sin and death (Heb 2:14–15). Sometimes this is called a cosmic drama, a drama in which Jesus immersed himself in the experience of humanity. Here, Jesus shared in our struggles and sufferings, and ultimately overcame and defeated the power of evil through his atonement, by establishing his kingdom. Together with penal substitution, Martin Luther also taught the Christus Victor theme. In his *Large Catechism* he wrote, "He [Christ] has redeemed me from sin, from the devil, from death, and all evil. For before I had no Lord nor King, but was captive under the power of the devil, condemned to death, enmeshed in sin and blindness."[1]

In 1931 a Swedish theologian, Gustaf Aulén, wrote a famous little book titled *Christus Victor: An Historical Study of the Three Main Types of the Idea of Atonement*. In his book he describes the central idea of the Christus Victor theme as God and his kingdom in a battle against the evil powers. These powers were on an all-out assault on humanity. The idea of atonement, Aulén argues, is that of a divine conflict and victory in which Christ the Victor fights and triumphs over the evil powers, those powers which hold humanity in bondage and inflict suffering. It is through Jesus Christ the Victor that God reconciles humanity and the world to himself. This battle is seen as a kind of cosmic battle and victory over the evil powers.[2]

While Gustaf Aulén popularized the Christus Victor theme in the twentieth century, today other theologians such as J. Denny Weaver, Gregory A. Boyd and N. T. Wright have emphasized and developed the Christus Victor theme, sometimes over and above penal substitution. The penal substitutionary view is often seen as too individualistic and unable to engage or address the problems of endless suffering and evil on a cosmic level. There have, therefore, been recent controversies on the issue of atonement. Steve Chalke and Alan Mann

---

1. Martin Luther, *The Large Catechism*, trans. F. Bente and W. H. T. Dau (St. Louis: Concordia, 1921), 111.

2. See Gustaf Aulén, *Christus Victor: An Historical study of the Three Main Types of the Idea of Atonement*, trans. A. G. Herbert (1931; Eugene: Wipf & Stock, 2003).

wrote a book, *The Lost Message of Jesus*, which criticized penal substitution, calling it "cosmic child abuse."[3] This led to a London Symposium on the theology of atonement five years later,[4] as well as the publication of various other books in response by theologians who advocated penal substitution and wished to respond to the controversy. Among others, these included *Pierced for Our Transgressions: Rediscovery of Penal Substitution* by Steve Jeffery, Michael Ovey and Andrew Sach, and *In My Place Condemned He Stood: Celebrating the Glory of Atonement* by J. I. Packer and Mark Dever.

Others have sought to find a combination of both penal substitution and the Christus Victor theme. In this book I argue that such a combination is evident throughout Scripture and most of church history, and perhaps most strikingly through Martin Luther's work. Some remarkable more recent publications which advocate such a combination of the two themes include Hans Boersma's book *Violence, Hospitality and the Cross: Reappropriating the Atonement Tradition*, Scot McKnight's *A Community Called Atonement* and Sinclair Ferguson's article "Christus Victor et Propitiator: The Death of Christ, Substitute and Conqueror." While I also advocate such a combination in the atonement, in this book we will look at it within an African perspective.

In the context of Christianity in Africa, the implications of such an atonement theology demonstrate that Christ's atonement is more than capable of dealing with African concerns and interests, offering liberty and hope. Penal substitution and the Christus Victor theme fulfil a profound need in African culture and spirituality.

Africa is a profoundly diverse continent; and so I shall address general African concepts and beliefs that apply across a wide range of African people groups.

Professor James Nkansah-Obrembong has argued that African evangelicals have not made full use of their resources in an effort to develop a truly African theology.[5] Africa needs a theology that is grounded in both the Scriptures and the theology of the church, and is profoundly meaningful for the African people. It is my prayer that *Spectacular Atonement* may offer a positive contribution to "a truly African theology."

3. Steve Chalke and Alan Mann, *The Lost Message of Jesus* (Grand Rapids: Zondervan, 2003), 182–83, 191–92.

4. See Derek Tidball, David Hilborn and Justin Thacker, eds., *The Atonement Debate: Papers from the London Symposium on the Theology of Atonement* (Grand Rapids: Zondervan, 2008).

5. James Nkansah-Obrembong, "The Contemporary Theological Situation in Africa: An Overview," *Evangelical Review of Theology* 31, no. 2 (2007): 140–50.

The very nature of Christian theology requires that theology developed by African Christians should also take the teachings of the wider Christian community into consideration. As a Ghanaian Proverb says, "One head does not contain all the wisdom." Nkansah-Obrembong has said that "theological ideas and theological formulation become more fruitful and relevant if they reflect the thought forms of the recipient's culture," and that much effort is needed to work towards a "comprehensive and systematic theology that is biblically and culturally relevant for the church in Africa."[6] A truly African theology needs "to reformulate or reinterpret the one biblical, historical, Judeo-Christian message in the idioms of the African peoples in response to the issues and concerns confronting African believers in their historical contexts."[7] In this book you will meet many African theologians whose writings are not as well known as they deserve to be. All of them have an important contribution to make towards an authentic African Christian theology. I have learned much from these African theologians, and I am sure you will too. I hope that by my introducing them to you, you will in your own time discover their theology and their writings.

Nevertheless, I believe that African Christians should also be exposed to a theology that is uniquely African. A theology that is their own.

---

6. Nkansah-Obrembong, "Contemporary Theological Situation," 140, 142–44, 149.

7. Nkansah-Obrembong, 140.

Part 1

Part 1

2

Atonement in Scripture

In this chapter I trace the biblical roots of the cross of Christ in both the Old and the New Testaments. I will show how the penal substitution and the Christus Victor themes are biblical themes of the atoning work of Christ. You will also discover how they are significant.

Old Testament

The story of the atonement begins very early in Scripture, in Genesis. Chapter 3 presents us with an account of humanity's rebellion against God through Adam and Eve's sin. They then find themselves in a terrible situation as a result of their disobedience and the devastating effects of sin. Genesis 3:15 reads, "I will put enmity between you and the woman, and between your offspring and her *offspring*; he shall bruise your head, and you shall bruise his heel" (emphasis mine). The word for "offspring" is singular in the Hebrew, the original language of the Old Testament. This has led many theologians through the centuries to see a connection between the "offspring" in Genesis 3:15 and Jesus.

Jesus, Mary's offspring, finds himself in conflict with Satan, the serpent. The gospels portray Jesus as conqueror over Satan and the evil spirits, most notably in his exorcisms (see Matt 8:16–17; 12:22–31; Mark 1:21–26, 29–34; 5:2–13; 9:15–29; 11:14–23). Yet Jesus's defeat of Satan was not without cost, for Jesus's "heel was bruised" when he was crucified. Ironically, Satan's "bruising" of Jesus on the cross was turned around, and Jesus became victorious over Satan, sin and death (Col 2:15 and Heb 2:14).

Later, in Exodus, the Hebrew people were enslaved by the Egyptians over the course of several centuries. God, however, worked through his servant Moses in order to free his people, and so he sent ten plagues against the Egyptians, the oppressors of the Hebrew people. Despite the suffering of the

Egyptians under such terrible plagues, they did not let the Hebrew people go until the final plague.

The final plague, however, would affect all the peoples of Egypt, including the Hebrews, although the Hebrews would be protected by means of a sacrificial ritual, the Passover. The Passover may be seen as an act of atonement which protected the Israelites from the anger of God which was set against the Egyptians, and in which he struck all the firstborn in the land of Egypt. In this account of the Passover, we notice clearly rudimentary penal substitution and Christus Victor themes.

At the Passover, just before the exodus out of Egypt, the people of Israel were told to take a lamb. Exodus 12:5 says that this lamb which they were to prepare and eat was to be "without blemish, a male a year old." The blood of the Passover lamb was not poured out onto an altar, but instead smeared onto the timber lintels and doorposts of the houses of the Hebrew families (Exod 12:7). This was a sign both for the Hebrew people and for God, as he would pass over those houses which had sacrificial blood smeared on their lintels and doorposts and so protect the people from harm (Exod 12:13). It was a life-saving rite! The sacrificial death of one victim, the lamb, offered life for many. Without the sacrificial lamb as a substitute, the Hebrew families would have suffered the same fate as the Egyptians, the deaths of their firstborn. Already in Exodus one can begin to see the penal substitution and Christus Victor themes in action.

God proclaims in Exodus 12:12, "For I will pass through the land of Egypt that night, and I will strike all the firstborn in the land of Egypt, both man and beast; and on all the gods of Egypt I will execute judgements." God's judgement was not only against Pharaoh, but also against the gods of Egypt. Although God's justice and judgement are most certainly being served, we should not be too quick to overlook the punishment and penalty aspects of the Passover story. The Hebrews had provided a substitute, a sacrifice of a lamb, in order to protect themselves from the coming judgement.

God's judgements and victory were unmatched as he judged Pharaoh and the gods of Egypt and delivered his people from the hands of the Egyptians. From then on the Hebrews would know the means of their deliverance and redemption: the blood of a sacrificed lamb as their substitute, making atonement for them. The lamb took the place of the firstborn of the Hebrew people and covered them from the destroyer.

Truly, this Passover lamb was the model of God's redemptive work in the Old Testament par excellence! Yet this redemptive model is developed in the New Testament to be indescribably superior. Jesus Christ in the New Testament becomes this lamb (John 1:29; 1 Pet 1:19): he becomes the sacrificial Passover lamb (1 Cor 5:7), offering atonement for us.

After the last plague, in which all the firstborn in Egypt died, including Pharaoh's firstborn, Pharaoh finally agreed to let his Hebrew slaves go. However, once they reached the shores of the Red Sea, they found themselves being pursued by the Egyptian army. Evidently, Pharaoh had had a change of mind. God does the unthinkable and miraculously parts the Red Sea, allowing a passage for the Israelites to successfully escape their enemies. While the Israelites were rescued, the Egyptian army drowned and was defeated. Moses, Miriam and the Israelites joyfully sang a victory psalm to God, for he had been victorious in freeing his people from slavery and destroying their oppressors (Exod 15:1–18). Thus the links between deliverance and the victorious warrior God are made evident.

Later in Exodus, in chapter 30 verse 10, we find the unmistakable theme of the atonement when Aaron is instructed to make atonement on the horns of the altar once a year. "With the blood of the sin offering of atonement he shall make atonement for it once in the year throughout your generations. It is most holy to the LORD" (Exod 30:10). The consecration of the altar introduces us to an atonement liturgy, as it were, and to themes of propitiation and appeasement by means of blood. This atoning sacrifice was different because, unlike the Passover lamb, it was an offering for the sin of the Hebrew people, and therefore was a sacrifice presented on an altar.

The atonement is fully spelled out in Leviticus 16: the Day of Atonement. Consider the penal substitutionary aspects here.

It is explained in Leviticus 16:16 that atonement is to be made in the Most Holy Place, because of the uncleanness of the Israelite people and their sins. Atonement had to be made on the altar that stood before God, by applying the blood from a bull and a goat to the horns of the altar (vv. 17b–18). Aaron was to lay his hands on a living goat's head, and then confess all the sins, iniquities and transgressions of the people of Israel. These were symbolically placed on the goat. The goat, carrying the sins of the people, was then led away into the wilderness or sometimes over a cliff (vv. 21–22). Atonement in the Old Testament rituals and sacrifices foreshadows an infinitely superior sacrifice in the New Testament. This superior sacrifice, as we shall see, provides redemption, freedom and forgiveness.

This superior sacrifice already comes into focus in Isaiah's magnificent messianic prophecy. The atoning themes in Isaiah 52:13 – 53:12 are not only significant for the Old Testament, but are vital for understanding atonement theology in the New Testament as well. In these verses the themes of penal substitution and Christus Victor are artfully woven together.

Isaiah's prophecy starts by describing how God's servant would act wisely, and that he would be lifted up and exalted (Isa 52:13). This, however, is contrasted with what follows. Verse 14 states that "many were astonished at you – his appearance was so marred, beyond human semblance, and his form beyond that of the children of mankind," and yet verse 15 proclaims that "kings shall shut their mouths because of him." Isaiah 53 develops this contrast where the servant is said to be "despised and rejected by men; a man of sorrows, and acquainted with grief" (53:3a). The reason for such sorrow is found in verse 4a: "Surely he has borne our griefs and carried our sorrows." The substitutionary idea in the word "carried" is obvious, bearing the consequences of another's sin.

Verse 4 describes the suffering and humiliation of the servant. This is important, because the servant carried the sufferings and sins of many. The verse continues to tell us that the servant was "smitten by God." Nevertheless, verse 5 tells us that it was because of this "chastisement" that we can have peace, and that we are healed by his stripes. The result or purpose of the servant's suffering was our welfare and peace.

In verse 6, Isaiah focuses on humanity, that it is *we* who have gone astray like sheep. All of us have turned and have gone our own way, and yet it was God who laid all our iniquities upon the servant! The imagery of the servant being the ritual sacrificial lamb is expressed in verse 7, and it is here that the language of the Day of Atonement is highlighted. The sins of the people were symbolically transferred to the scapegoat. We are reminded in verses 7 and 8 that the servant suffered oppression and judgement. Yet the servant, as the prophet Isaiah explains, was stricken *for* the transgressions of God's people. Here the substitutionary theme becomes obvious.

The parallels in verse 9 between the death and burial of the servant and Jesus's death and burial are unmistakable (Matt 27:57–60). This servant who experienced oppression and affliction was innocent and without violence. Even though he was undeserving of judgement, verse 10 tells us that it was the will of God to crush him (or to oppress him) and to put him to grief. We should read these verses in light of the latter part of verse 10. The servant offers his life up as an offering *for our* guilt, and it is this offering which God looks upon favourably when he sees it, prolonging the servant's days; and "the will of the LORD shall prosper in his hand" (53:10b).

The result of the suffering mentioned in Isaiah 53:11 is the servant's satisfaction, for he knows that by his bearing the iniquities of many, many shall be accounted righteous.

After a detailed description of the servant's rejection, affliction and death, a change of situation emerges in verse 12 where the servant's triumph is celebrated. Note the victory language in this verse: "Therefore I will divide him a portion with the many, and he shall divide the spoil with the strong." This anticipates the Christus Victor theme. This servant's path to victory was certainly very different from any other! As reward for this victory, God divides for the servant a portion with the many, and will divide the spoil with the strong. Oswalt explains that this is a "picture of a victory parade with the servant, of all people, marching in the role of conqueror, bringing home the spoils of conquest."[1] Such a victory has been achieved "because he poured out his soul to death and was numbered with the transgressors" (53:12b).

The substitutionary theme is highlighted again in verse 12c: "yet he bore the sin of many and makes intercession for the transgressors." It is important for us to understand in the light of verse 10 that the servant took upon *himself* the sin of the world, and like the scapegoat in Leviticus 16:22 carries those sins away from us.

While the word "atonement" does not feature in Isaiah 52:13 – 53:12, substitutionary and atoning language is implied throughout, notably in how the servant suffers on behalf of many, how he is like a lamb led to the slaughter, and in the fact that he bears our sin and guilt. Once again the metaphor of sacrifice emphasizes the victorious nature of the servant's suffering and death. This is a unique instance, because normally guilt cannot be transferred to another (Ezek 18:20), and neither can a man "ransom another, or give to God the price of his life, for the ransom of their life is costly and can never suffice" (Ps 49:7–8). This servant is not an ordinary man! His uniqueness surely points to a messianic figure, Jesus Christ. The language in Isaiah 52:13 – 53:12, then, clearly draws substitutionary suffering and Christus Victor themes together, into a spectacular atonement.

New Testament

The drama of the atonement in the Old Testament eagerly anticipated an infinitely superior atonement in the New Testament. Here, the obscure figure about whom we read in Genesis 3:15 and the suffering servant in Isaiah reveals himself to be the saviour of humanity and indeed the entire cosmos.

---

1. John N. Oswalt, *The Book of Isaiah Chapters 40–66*, The New International Commentary on the Old Testament (Grand Rapids: Eerdmans, 1998), 405.

The Gospels and John's Writings

Much of the atonement theology in the gospels demonstrates Old Testament continuity in Jesus's own messianic understanding, especially with respect to Isaiah's suffering servant. Further, as we shall see, Jesus's mission was not the political one for which his Jewish friends had hoped. Instead he proclaimed a personal salvation in the context of a "cosmic struggle" against demonic forces. The African theologian Ogbu Kalu noted that "Jesus' ministry was very much a cosmic battle in which he rescued humanity from evil powers."[2] Jesus was at the centre of this "cosmic battle" against the forces of evil.

Corresponding to Isaiah's suffering servant, Jesus clarified his reason for suffering in Matthew 20:28, saying that "the Son of Man came not to be served but to serve, and to give his life as a *ransom for many*" (emphasis mine). Jesus's giving up his life for many is an echo of Isaiah 49:6, where God says that he will make his servant a light to all nations, and that God's salvation will reach to the ends of the earth. Isaiah 53:12 also tells how the servant gives up his life to death, bearing the sins of many. Given these passages, it seems possible that Jesus was interpreting his own life, death and resurrection in the light of Isaiah's suffering servant.[3]

This ransom price was to be completely paid. The word "for" in "ransom for many" highlights the idea of an exchange being made. The idea of ransom was commonly used in the ancient Graeco-Roman world, but perhaps one of the most useful contexts in which to understand ransom for our purposes is the one presented by the New Testament scholar D. A. Carson. He explains that the "ransom" was the purchase price for freeing slaves; there is good evidence, Carson believes, that the concept of "purchase price" is usually implied in the New Testament use of ransom. In the ancient Graeco-Roman world, redemption language was common economic language, especially for the redeeming of slaves. Sometimes people might become slaves because of dire personal economic circumstances, selling themselves, and perhaps also their families, into slavery. But if there were friends or family members who were caring and wealthy, they could make arrangements with the owners of the slaves and buy them back out of slavery. This was called "redemption." According to Carson, this worked by paying the price for the slave to a pagan temple. Some of this money went to the temple priests, and the temple in turn

---

2. Ogbu Kalu, *African Pentecostalism: An Introduction* (Oxford: Oxford University Press, 2008), 182.

3. D. A. Carson, *Matthew*, vol. 8 of *The Expositor's Bible Commentary*, General ed. F. E. Gaebelein (Grand Rapids: Zondervan, 1984), 434.

would pay the rest to the slave owner. The ownership of the slave was then transferred from the slave owner to the temple's deity. This meant that if you were a slave to a temple god, you were basically a freed person, but you still held the status of being a slave.[4] Throughout the New Testament, the word "ransom" is used metaphorically for setting people free from sin and its penalty as the cost of Jesus's sacrificial death on the cross.

Jesus offers not only a transaction, but a substitution by way of redemption. Here we are able to observe hints of penal substitutionary atonement and Christus Victor themes. In this way the ransoming in Matthew 20:28 engages with the whole biblical story as well as with the redemptive concepts found in the ancient Graeco-Roman world. When we turn to the letters of Paul below, we will see that by buying us back, as it were, God frees us as slaves, and in so doing reconciles us back to himself. He frees us from the evil powers that once held us in bondage (Rom 3:21–26; Gal 5:1; Col 1:19–22; 2:13–20).

As we read the gospels we see that Jesus's ministry was marked by healings and exorcisms. It becomes evident that the centrality of his ministry was warfare – warfare against evil spiritual forces. In 1 John 3:8b, John writes, "The reason the Son of God appeared was to destroy the works of the devil."[5] This is at the very centre of the cross of Christ.

The image of Jesus giving himself up as a ransom for many is beautifully fleshed out (pun intended) in the Lord's Supper (Matt 26:26–29). Here Jesus's death is identified as the climax of his self-sacrificing service in ministry. Jesus took bread and after having blessed it, he broke it and gave it to his disciples, saying, "Take, eat, this is my body" (v. 26). He then took the cup and after having given thanks, he gave it to them, saying,

> Drink of it, all of you, for this is my blood of the covenant, which is *poured out* for many for the forgiveness of sins. I tell you I will not drink again of this fruit of the vine until that day when I drink it new with you in my Father's kingdom. (vv. 27b–29; emphasis mine)

The words "poured out" remind us of the blood poured out on the altar as a sacrificial atonement in the Old Testament. The purpose of Jesus shedding his blood for many is marked by the word "for": the forgiveness of sins.

---

4. D. A. Carson, *Scandalous: The Cross and the Resurrection of Jesus* (Wheaton: Crossway, 2010), 58–59.

5. See Gregory A. Boyd, *God at War: The Bible and Spiritual Warfare* (Downers Grove: InterVarsity Press, 1997), 249.

The Lord's Supper is a New Testament Passover. Jesus, according to the first three gospels, celebrated the Passover with his disciples on the night of his betrayal, and he died during the Passover. According to John's gospel, Jesus died on the afternoon of the Passover, just as the Passover lambs were being sacrificed in the temple. John clearly represents the crucifixion in Passover language (see John 19). It is no surprise then that Paul in 1 Corinthians 5:7 calls Jesus "our Passover lamb."

The Lord's Supper in Matthew 26:26–29 shows us that penal substitution is a new-covenant extension of the Old Testament Passover along with the temple's rituals and sacrifices. As we read in verse 28, it is not our blood but Jesus's blood that is poured out for the forgiveness of our sins; in this way it is penal substitution. The Lord's Supper, therefore, ties all of Scripture together in a single event, stretching back into the Old Testament and yet anticipating a future kingdom, a future hope, a hope in Christ Jesus.

Christ rescuing us from sin is by no means insignificant. When John the Baptist speaks to his disciples about Jesus, the one who will come after him, you can almost see the wonder in John's eyes and the trembling of his knees as he tells them, "I baptize with water, but among you stands one you do not know, even he who comes after me, the strap of whose sandal I am not worthy to untie" (John 1:26–27). The next day, John, seeing Jesus approaching him, proclaims in a moment of stunning adoration, "Behold, the Lamb of God, who takes away the sin of the world!" (John 1:29b). John's insight here is astonishing! He sees Jesus as a sacrificial lamb, perhaps as the Passover lamb of the new covenant. Jesus is the atoning saviour of the world who sacrifices himself so that our sins may be removed for ever. The Gospel of John picks up on various themes to develop the idea of Jesus being the Passover lamb offering a sacrifice: first, as we noted, Jesus's death occurred during the time of the Passover sacrifice (John 18:28; 19:14); second, both the hyssop and the basin were at the cross during Jesus's death (John 19:29; see Exod 12:22); third, blood flowed from Jesus's side and its witness is emphasized (John 19:31–35; see Exod 12:13); and lastly, none of Jesus's bones were broken (John 19:31–37; Exod 12:46).[6]

The Passover lamb in Jewish thought was a tremendously important sacrifice. For Jews, the sacrifice of a lamb, particularly in light of the Passover lamb, contained powerful symbolism attached to the ideas of deliverance, which implies victory, and messianic salvation. As we saw earlier, the Passover

---

6. Joel B. Green and Mark D. Baker, *Recovering the Scandal of the Cross: Atonement in New Testament and Contemporary Contexts* (Wheaton: IVP Academic, 2000), 78.

lamb provided protection from the final plague visited on the Egyptians, when many of their firstborn perished. And so it is the sacrifice of the Passover lamb that joins the themes of victory and salvation.

While there were many sacrificial lambs in the Old Testament, Jesus is the lamb par excellence! (See also Isa 53, especially v. 7.) Jesus is a lamb superior to all the others that were ever sacrificed since unlike other lambs he takes away the sin of the world. "Sin" in John 1:29 is singular, and therefore John is referring to the world's sin, rather than just to some sins of some individuals. This lamb is spectacular, and the scope of his atoning death is greater than you and I have ever imagined!

But there is also a cosmic struggle, a battle, in the death of this lamb. The death of Jesus with his subsequent resurrection has meaning both for the physical conflict with the Jewish authorities, and for the spiritual conflict which was played out in Jesus's ministry. Consider Jesus's battle with the evil spirits. A heated discussion emerges in Mark 3:22–27 between the scribes from Jerusalem, who were saying of Jesus, "He is possessed by Beelzebul" and "by the prince of demons he casts out the demons" (v. 22b). Jesus responds by showing how illogical their thinking is: "How can Satan cast out Satan?" (v. 23b). He calls them to give careful thought to their accusation. How can a kingdom or even a household that is divided against itself still stand? Therefore, if Satan rises up against himself and is divided, how can he stand? Surely he will destroy himself (vv. 24–26)! Jesus then begins speaking about himself in verse 27: "But no one can enter a strong man's house and plunder his goods, unless he first binds the strong man. Then indeed he may plunder his house." The kingdom of Satan is therefore not being destroyed from within, but rather an external power is attacking it and freeing its captives, proclaiming the coming of a new, very different kingdom, God's kingdom. Certainly, the kingdom of God *is* at hand (Mark 1:15)!

Jesus makes it plain in verse 27 that only someone who is stronger than the strong man (Satan) can enter his house. The phrase "unless he first binds the strong man" has a somewhat future emphasis, especially given that Revelation 20:1–3 tells us how Satan will be bound for a thousand years. Jesus was speaking about himself; he is the one who is more powerful than the strong man, for it was he who cast out demons and healed the sick. Consequently, Mark 3:22–27 displays vibrant Christus Victor imagery where Jesus describes vividly the cosmic struggle in which he is victorious. It is Jesus who binds the "strong man."

Then, in verse 28, Jesus announces "total forgiveness," and by implication those who have sinned will be released from the "legal" consequences of their sin. However, while Jesus offers total forgiveness, salvation and forgiveness do not come without repentance (Luke 5:32; 24:47; 2 Cor 7:10; 2 Pet 3:9).

In Luke 4:33–36 we read of Jesus's cosmic struggle with the forces of evil (see Mark 1:21–28 for the same incident). Jesus entered a synagogue where there was an evil spirit which cried out to him, "Ha! What have you to do with us, Jesus of Nazareth? Have you come to destroy us? I know who you are – the Holy One of God." Verse 33 tells us that this was a single demon, and so when it asks "Have you come to destroy *us*?" it is probably referring to itself as well as the possessed man. One gets a sense of the cosmic battle. Jesus has power and authority over evil spirits, and they know it! Interestingly, Darrell Bock explains that the Jews understood that demonic power would be defeated in the age of the Messiah, and that it would be then that the "die of cosmic confrontation [was] cast." The Jews also believed that the messianic victor would be revealed through battle.[7] Jesus had in mind here more than a single exorcism. Jesus Christ has in fact purposed to utterly destroy and conquer the whole demonic realm and free humanity, rescuing them from demonic oppression and their sin (Col 1:13–14; 2:15).

This conquering Christ is also pictured in John's vision in Revelation 5:5–13. I well remember studying these few verses late one night. No words could express my surprise as I discovered the meaning of this passage. I felt like a man who had stumbled upon something too beautiful for words to describe, as wonder filled my soul. I shall try to communicate something of what I discovered that night.

In Revelation 5:5–13 John records a vision of a brilliant display of symbolism and paradox. In this vision John begins to weep, for there is no one to open the seals of the sacred scroll (5:1–4). In verse 5 a heavenly elder comforts John, "Behold, the Lion of the tribe of Judah, the Root of David, has conquered, so that he can open the scroll and its seven seals." "Open," or in the Greek "*to* open," indicates that this is the result of Jesus having conquered – that is, "*therefore* he can open the scroll." Similarly, when in John 19:30 Jesus cries out, "It is finished," John stresses the completed action of Jesus and so uses the perfect tense for "it is finished" – that is, Jesus's work on the cross was complete, and yet has recurring consequences into the future.

The messianic victory described in Revelation is a final and complete victory, for Christ is the victorious Lion (Rev 5:5)! Because he has conquered, only Jesus, who is "the Lion of the tribe of Judah, the Root of David" (see also

7. Darrell L. Bock, *Luke 1:1 – 9:50*, Baker Exegetical Commentary on the New Testament (Grand Rapids: Baker Academic, 1994), 431, 435.

Isa 11:1 and Rom 15:12), is worthy to open the seven seals of the scroll and reveal its contents.

The paradox emerges in verse 6, where this lion is also a lamb – a slain lamb! There is a contradiction in Christ. He conquers, but the means of his victory is his sacrificial death. Instead of a victorious lion, John now sees "a Lamb standing, as though it had been slain" (or "slaughtered" in Greek). The lion of verse 5 is a lamb with seven horns and seven eyes, "which are the seven spirits of God sent out into all the earth" (v. 6). In John's gospel Christ is identified as a lamb, and in John's Revelation the "Lamb" becomes a title for Jesus Christ. The imagery in the vision of Christ as the slaughtered Lamb connects Christ's sacrificial death to the Passover lamb in the Old Testament.

The comparative particle "as," in "a Lamb standing, *as* though it had been slain," does not, however, mean that the Lamb simply *appeared* as if it had been slaughtered; instead what John is saying is that the Lamb who was slaughtered is now alive! But this slaughtered Lamb in Revelation 5:6 who is the crucified Christ is not a victim: he is the all-powerful Victor! His seven horns are a symbol of perfect might, and his seven eyes a symbol of perfect knowledge.

The Lamb then went and took the scroll, and in this cosmic liturgy the four living creatures and the twenty-four elders fell face down before the Lamb (5:7–8), and they began to sing a new song: "Worthy are you to take the scroll and to open its seals, for you were slain, and by your blood you ransomed people for God from every tribe and language and people and nation" (vv. 9b–10).

This song gives us three reasons why Jesus was worthy to take the scroll and open its seals. First, because he was slain. It was by means of Jesus's crucifixion that he was able to purchase humanity's redemption. Second, because Jesus, through his atoning work, ransomed people for God from every tribe, language, people and nation. This was a fulfilment of God's purpose to bless every nation through the seed of Abraham (Gen 12:2–3; 13:14–16; 17:1–8). Further, Revelation 5:9b reads, "By your blood you ransomed people for God." Jesus secured the rights for us by paying a price. The price was infinitely valuable: the death of Christ Jesus. This shows the costliness and seriousness of our sin against God.

The imagery and implications here in Revelation are *far* richer than merely "freeing slaves"! We saw earlier how a ransomed slave would become the property or slave of the pagan deity of a temple after the ransom had been paid. But when Christ ransoms us for God, we do not become slaves to a pagan deity, as in the Graeco-Roman world. Instead, Christ makes *us* priests! He makes us a kingdom in which we become priests of God, and one day we shall reign on earth with Christ (Rev 5:10). No doubt this would have had a profound impact on John's first readers, who would have been familiar with Graeco-Roman culture.

The third reason why Jesus was worthy to take the scroll and open its seals is that by means of the cross Jesus achieved a victory for his people (Rev 5:5). Jesus conquered death itself.

N. T. Wright says that at the point of Jesus's crucifixion he presented himself as the slain Passover lamb in the face of all the satanic forces allied against him, together with hostile humanity and their institutions. Raging against the Christ, they "hurled their worst at him," but by absorbing this he simultaneously defeated them and triumphed in divine love, and in so doing carried out "the perfect will of his Father."[8] Through the atoning work of the cross, Christ made the satanic and hostile forces of humanity agents of victory, turning evil against itself and ultimately leading evil to its own ruin.[9] Like the Passover theme in the Lord's Supper, which refers back to the sacrificial lamb before the exodus out of Egypt, Revelation 5:5–10 shows us the hope of a kingdom that begins now, through the blood of this new Passover lamb, Jesus Christ.

Revelation presented us with a fascinating paradox where Jesus is spoken of as a lion in one verse and then as a lamb in the next. In his gospel, John presents another paradox, this time with Jesus as the good shepherd (John 10:14).

In John 10 Jesus is holding a conversation with the Pharisees and the Jews and refers to himself as the good shepherd. Jesus knows that he will endanger his life and endure suffering in order to rescue his sheep. He gives himself up, substituting his life in death for the lives of his sheep. Make no mistake, Jesus was not compelled to give up his life for the sake of his sheep. No, he did it of his own free will; no one had the power to take his life from him without his consent (v. 18). Jesus also had the power and authority to take his life up again in resurrection (vv. 15, 17–18). These verses make it plain that Jesus had the freedom of choice, including the option to sacrifice himself in death.

Yet verse 18 also tells us that Jesus sacrificed himself in obedience to his Father. As a member of the Holy Trinity, Jesus is in perfect harmony with the Father. Jesus's death was not an end in itself, but pointed to his resurrection. His death was in order that he might rise again and ultimately be glorified (12:27–28), giving eternal life to his sheep. The shepherd's death, then, was not a defeat but a victory, for on the third day Jesus would be raised from the dead.

8. N. T. Wright, *Surprised by Hope: Rethinking Heaven, the Resurrection, and the Mission of the Church* (New York: HarperOne, 2008), 68.

9. Wright, *Surprised by Hope*, 68.

Jesus speaks about his death as a victory in John 12:31–32, highlighting his confrontation with Satan, proclaiming, "Now is the judgement of this world; now will the ruler of this world be cast out." The "ruler of this world" is a reference to Satan. At the fall in Genesis 3, humanity subjected themselves and all creation to the evil forces that are in opposition to God.[10] Gregory Boyd says that the old "prince of this world" has been "cast out" and a new prince, Jesus Christ, "a legitimate ruler, has been enthroned in his place."[11] The former prince held humanity in bondage, sin and suffering, but the new prince offers, at no cost, forgiveness of sins through repentance.[12]

Jesus proclaimed, "And I, when I am lifted up from the earth, will draw all people to myself" (John 12:32). Jesus's death and resurrection marked the beginning of the end of satanic rule, ultimately bringing about Satan's defeat. We read in Revelation 20:10 that Satan's defeat at the present time is incomplete, but at the consummation of the age it will be final. This confrontation with Satan is also expressed in one of John's letters, 1 John 3:8b: "The reason the Son of God appeared was to destroy the works of the devil."

Christ's atoning work pays the penalty for our sin as a substitution, and so earlier in 1 John 3 John writes, "You know that he appeared to *take away sins*, and in him there is no sin" (v. 5; emphasis mine). Penal substitutionary atonement and Christus Victor go together here. When these parts are seen together, the atonement is nothing short of magnificent.

Considering the word "propitiation" in 1 John 2:2, Hengel explains its meaning in the early Greek period as the sacrifice of an individual person for the good of the community. For example, the sacrifice might be to appease the anger of the gods. Such sacrificial death usually did not rest on an individual's own decision, but was required by a god or goddess to atone for the people, so that he or she would not be angry towards them.[13]

J. I. Packer contrasts the propitiation required from pagan gods with that of the God of the Bible: "In paganism, man propitiates his gods, and religion becomes a form of commercialism and, indeed, of bribery. In Christianity, God propitiates his wrath by his own action."[14] John Stott makes the same points clear. First, God's wrath is not arbitrary or unpredictable. It bears no

---

10. Boyd, *God at War*, 111, 181.

11. Boyd, 245.

12. Boyd, 245.

13. Martin Hengel, *The Atonement: The Origins of the Doctrine in the New Testament*, trans. J. Bowden (Eugene: Wipf & Stock, 1981), 19, 87.

14. J. I. Packer and Mark Dever, *In My Place Condemned He Stood: Celebrating the Glory of Atonement* (Wheaton: Crossway, 2007), 36.

resemblance to the unpredictable passions and personal vengefulness of the pagan deities. Instead, it is his settled, controlled, holy hatred towards all evil. Second, the means by which his wrath is averted is not a bribe, either from us or from a third party. On the contrary, the initiative in the propitiation is entirely God's.[15] God makes the propitiation, not us!

Paul's Writings

This brings us to the apostle Paul, among the many terms which he applies to the death of Jesus, he also uses "propitiation." Paul writes in Romans 3:24–25 that we "are justified by his grace as a gift, through the redemption that is in Christ Jesus, whom God put forward as a propitiation by his blood, to be received by faith. This was to show God's righteousness, because in his divine forbearance he had passed over former sins." Here the idea of redemption becomes apparent once again. In Romans 3:24 Paul refers to the act of "redemption" for those who have been justified by grace as a gift and have placed their faith in Christ as their Lord and Saviour. Jesus, having died on the cross, offered himself as a propitiation, and satisfied the holy wrath of God which was set against us (Rom 3:25–26; Heb 2:17). God sent his Son as an atonement, as a propitiation, for our sins, and yet it was also a dramatic expression of God's love for humankind and creation (1 John 4:10). It was at the cross that God displayed his justice and his condemnation of sin, and in the same event he provided a means of atonement for the justification of sinners.

Without Jesus's atoning work on the cross, all people would stand under God's judgement and would experience his anger. But a new righteousness has now appeared in the history of redemption to address our terrible situation. In Romans 3:21, Paul shows us that we can have a righteousness that is not our own, and that is available to all on the condition of faith. We need to put our faith in Christ as our Lord and Saviour, and then he gives us *his* righteousness.

In Paul's letter to the Galatians, he shows how Christ's atoning work is a redemption from a curse. To begin, Paul writes in no uncertain terms that those who rely on the works of the law are under a curse, reminding us, "Cursed be everyone who does not abide by all things written in the Book of the Law, and do them" (Gal 3:10b; see Deut 26:27).

Galatians 3:13 expresses penal substitution beautifully: "Christ redeemed us from the curse of the law by becoming a curse for us – for it is written,

---

15. John Stott, *The Letters of John: An Introduction and Commentary*, Tyndale New Testament Commentary 19, rev. ed. (Grand Rapids: Eerdmans), Logos library system.

'Cursed is everyone who is hanged on a tree'" (see Deut 21:23). In Deuteronomy 28 we read about the blessings and curses – blessings for those who faithfully obey God and do all his commandments, and curses for those who disobey God. The curses are terrifying, and as we read further in the Old Testament we see how many disobeyed God and how these curses came into effect. Yet there is redemption in Christ, who by dying on the cross liberates us so that we might have his obedience. In Galatians 3:13, Jesus frees us from the curse that hung over us, by becoming a curse *for* us. Christ broke the curse that was placed on humankind. Logically, a curse spoken by God is more terrible than a curse spoken by a person or even by a spirit. Surely all curses ever spoken by human beings or spirits, past, present and future, were destroyed in that instant of Christ's atoning work on the cross, even though this verse is speaking specifically about the curse of the law. Ever since the time of Christ's death, any curse spoken to those who are redeemed by Christ has been utterly powerless! Such curses are cancelled in Christ. In other words, those who are in Christ through his redemption are not subject to any curse. Christ purchased our freedom by taking the curse – all curses – upon himself, by becoming the object of a curse in our stead.

The main focus in Galatians 3:13, however, is our relation to the law, and its curse as slavery. The idea once again is the practice of ransoming in the ancient Graeco-Roman world. The liberation from the curse of the law in verse 13 provides a real and legal freedom, which ensures that any legal claim of the law is satisfied for ever in Christ Jesus.

Not only has Christ overcome curses through his spectacular atonement, but he has also overcome evil spirits. We see this when Paul addresses the Ephesian church. Ephesians 1:20–30 places all the spirits of the spirit world in proper relation to Christ and to the Christian believer. These verses seem to be Paul's interpretation of Psalm 110, as he describes the spiritual forces which are now made subject to Jesus Christ (see Matt 26:64; Mark 12:36; Luke 20:41–44). Paul tells us that when God raised Christ up from the dead and seated him at his right hand in the heavenly places, this position is far above all rule, power and authority of the spirit world, and above all dominions.

The African theologian Professor Yusufu Turaki offers some helpful commentary on Ephesians 1:20–23; he proclaims that the fallen world has now been handed to Christ by God the Father because of his victory and triumph at the cross. The cross has become the symbol of his kingdom, his power and his rulership over all the earth. It was through the cross that Christ dethroned Satan and thereby subjected all principalities and powers to himself.[16]

Referring back to the fall and the fallen world of Genesis 3, Paul reminds us in another letter, Colossians 2:12–14, that we were once spiritually dead in sin, but that now our sin has been forgiven, on account of Christ's atoning work on the cross having satisfied the legal demands by cancelling the record of our debt. Paul's atonement theology is interesting here because verses 12–14 discuss the legal aspects of the atonement and then, in verse 15, Paul emphasizes the Christus Victor theme, saying, "He [God] disarmed the rulers and authorities and put them to open shame, by triumphing over them in him." I appreciate the *African Bible Commentary*'s helpful historical background on the rulers and authorities mentioned in these verses; it explains that they are the defeated enemies of God, being dragged along in Christ's procession. In the Roman world, "when a city surrendered to a victorious general, the conquerors would stage a victory parade at which they would display their conquered enemies and all the goods they had plundered."[17]

Notice God's irony here: it is while Jesus hangs on the cross in a seemingly hopeless situation that he leads a triumphal procession of captured rulers in a similar fashion to the way a Roman emperor would have led his captives.

These evil spirits, however, have not, as yet, been completely destroyed. They still continue to exist, having power to afflict and influence as they grope about in rage in Christ's triumphal procession. They are nevertheless powerless, unable to affect Christians who are in union with Christ and under his lordship.

In 1 Corinthians 15:20–28, the apostle Paul wrote about the Christus Victor theme in terms of the resurrection of the dead. Even though Christ is proclaimed as having being raised from the dead, the Christians in the Corinthian church were suggesting that there was no resurrection, at least in terms of humanity's resurrection (15:12). Paul argued that in fact not only was Jesus raised from the dead, but he was "the firstfruits of those who have fallen asleep" (v. 20). That is, others would be resurrected (raised to life) after him, because just as through one man came death, so by another man came life, or resurrection from the dead. Christ was raised first as the firstfruits, and then the rest of humanity will be resurrected at his coming (vv. 20–21 and 23).

Paul reasons in verse 22, "For as in Adam all die, so also in Christ shall all be made alive." Death became a reality for humanity as a result of the

16. Yusufu Turaki, *The Uniqueness of Jesus Christ* (Nairobi: WordAlive, 2006), 64.

17. Tokunboh Adeyemo, Gen. ed., *Africa Bible Commentary* (Nairobi: WordAlive, 2006), 1453.

disobedience of the first man, for all humanity is included in Adam with respect to sin and death. Just as physical death became a reality as a result of humanity's fall (Gen 3), so resurrection will be a future reality because of the obedience of Jesus Christ. At the beginning of the old creation, Adam brought death, but at the beginning of the new creation, Jesus will bring life through bodily resurrection.

Our future resurrection and Christ's return are the climax of Christ's ultimate victory, for it is then that he will "deliver the kingdom to God the Father after destroying every rule and every authority and power" (1 Cor 15:24). No doubt this is a reference to both political and spiritual powers that are in opposition to Christ and his rule.

But for now, as Paul says in verse 25, Jesus "must reign until he has put all his enemies under his feet." Christ is currently the reigning King, but on his return he will utterly destroy all evil forces, even death itself, which stand against him, and will do so in fulfilment of Psalm 110:1, which reads, "The LORD said to my Lord: 'Sit at my right hand, until I make your enemies your footstool.'"

Hebrews

Throughout much of the Epistle to the Hebrews, the atoning work of Christ is expressed in relation to his high-priestly office. Turaki offers us a helpful start by considering the theological method used in this epistle. He notes how the atoning work of Christ can be applied to the relation of Jesus Christ to the cultures and religions of the world, and particularly to the cultures and religions of Africa. The Epistle to the Hebrews "bases its appeal to the Jewish Christians on the 'superiority' of the Messiah Jesus over the Judaic system," and so, too, its appeal to African Christians.[18] Peter Nyende makes a similar observation. He writes that if Jewish mediatorial figures are employed metaphorically to assist the audiences of Hebrews to understand Christ as the mediator, "then there is no reason why ancestors should not be used as such to conceive and speak of Christ as the mediator in Africa."[19]

Beginning in Hebrews 2:14–15, the author of the letter states that "the children," that is, humanity, are by nature flesh and blood, and that Christ chose to partake of the same through his incarnation. Then the purpose of

---

18. Turaki, *Uniqueness of Jesus Christ*, 106–7.

19. Peter Nyende, "Hebrews' Christology and Its Contemporary Apprehension in Africa," *Neotestamentica* 41, no. 2 (2007): 378.

Christ's incarnation is given: "that through death he might destroy the one who has the power of death, that is, the devil, and deliver all those who through fear of death were subject to lifelong slavery" (2:14b–15). This is not to say that the devil has ceased to exist. Rather, power and authority are now in the hands of the Victor, Jesus. Verse 17 reads, "Therefore [Jesus] had to be made like his brothers in every respect, so that he might become a merciful and faithful high priest in the service of God, to make propitiation for the sins of the people." Here we have propitiation again, whereby Christ pays a ransom on our behalf, turning God's anger away from us. The themes of penal substitution and Christus Victor are complementary in this passage.

In Hebrews 9:1–10, the author talks about the Old Testament temple arrangements. In verse 9b, he tells us that all these ceremonial laws "cannot perfect the conscience of the worshipper." Rather, they merely dealt with food, ceremonial washings, and other regulations that were enforced on the body, waiting for the time of the new order. Verses 11–15 present us with a description of this "new order" in light of the rituals and sacrifices of the Old Testament. The new order is the reshaping of the old, whereby the old covenant makes way for the new. F. F. Bruce said it well when he wrote that the old covenant was "the shadow to the substance, the outward and earthly copy to the inward and heavenly reality."[20]

The author of Hebrews brings this new order into focus with the appearance of Jesus Christ in verse 11 "as a high priest of the good things to come, . . . through the greater and more perfect tent" (ESV margin). This "tent" is, of course, greater than Moses's tabernacle which symbolized the old covenant and all the rituals and sacrifices that were associated with it; this "greater and more perfect tent" is a heavenly tabernacle in the very presence of God (see Heb 8:1–2). The high-priestly action of Christ is comparable to the rituals of the Day of Atonement, but it is greater and more spectacular. Now that Christ has appeared, the Old Testament rituals and sacrifices have been made redundant. A perfect, permanent and final sacrifice is now found in Jesus's death on the cross.

The picture of Jesus as the high priest develops in Hebrews 9:12. Here Jesus entered "once for all into the holy places," not by using blood from a sacrificial animal, but his own blood! The blood of Christ, the God-man himself, obtains eternal redemption. Blood from any other being could never obtain eternal salvation. The sacrificial blood must be the blood of a perfect being, and yet

---

20. F. F. Bruce, *The Epistle to the Hebrews*, The New International Commentary on the New Testament, rev. ed. (Grand Rapids: Eerdmans, 1990), Logos library system.

also the blood of a human, because it was humanity which rebelled against God. Only Christ, who is both God and man, could offer up such a sacrifice.

Christ is the sole redeemer; none other is able to secure redemption. This redemption is both eternal and infinite. The payment of this redemption price has permanent consequences, not only in that those of us who put our faith in Christ have eternal salvation, but also in that the cost was of infinite worth. God, in Christ Jesus, chose to take on human flesh while still remaining God for ever. Christ took on human flesh not only for the thirty-three years of his time on earth, but for eternity. Christ's nature as both God and man dates from his human conception and is permanent.

In Hebrews 9:13, the phrase "for if" contrasts the power and worth of Jesus's blood with that of the blood of goats and bulls and the sprinkling of defiled persons with the ashes of a heifer for the purification of the flesh. Continuing in verse 14, the author interprets Jesus's death in light of the Old Testament sacrifices, again demonstrating the superior quality of Christ's sacrificial blood and the new covenant as superior to the old. This consecration by Jesus's blood is irreversible and effective for ever, and without blood there is no forgiveness of sins (Matt 16:28; Eph 1:6; Heb 10:17–19).

The author reaches the climax of his comparison of the blood of Christ and the blood of Old Testament sacrifices with the words "how much more": "how much more will the blood of Christ, who through the eternal Spirit offered himself without blemish to God, purify our conscience from dead works to serve the living God" (9:14). Sacrifice, clearly, is central to the Letter to the Hebrews. While we have seen in earlier discussions that Jesus's sacrifice offers propitiation, in these verses from chapter 9 we see how such a sacrifice also offers cleansing – cleansing from our sins and "our conscience from dead works."

Jesus offered his blood to God as an unblemished sacrifice; not as an ordinary human being, or even as a martyr, but as the Christ, the Son of God. His atoning death was therefore final and absolute. The implications of Christ's sacrifice for traditional Africans are remarkable. Our redemption is found not in ceremony or sacrificial rituals, but in Christ's perfect sacrifice alone.

Peter's Writings

Like other authors of Scripture, the apostle Peter explores the concepts of ransoming and Jesus as a sacrificial lamb. In 1 Peter 1:17 Peter speaks about God's impartial judgement, and he goes on to remind his readers that they have been ransomed: "knowing that you were ransomed from the futile ways inherited from your forefathers, not with perishable things such as silver or gold, but with the precious blood of Christ, like that of a lamb without blemish or spot" (vv. 18–19). Peter has in mind a freedom from the empty way of life inherited from our ancestors, achieved through a ransom – the price paid by Christ. This precious blood is said to be "like that of a lamb without blemish or spot" (v. 19). Peter compares the blood of Christ to the blood of the Passover lamb.

Peter develops his atonement theology further in 1 Peter 2:23–24, where he makes frequent reference to Isaiah 53. He writes that when Christ was reviled, or hated, he did not hate in return, and even when he suffered to the point of death, Jesus did not threaten (see Isa 53:7, 9).

Peter writes in 1 Peter 2:24, "He himself bore our sins in his body on the tree, that we might die to sin and live to righteousness. By his wounds you have been healed" (Paul makes the same reference in Gal 3:13: Jesus bore our sin and our curse while he hung on a "tree," the cross). "By his wounds you have been healed" is significant because it refers to the suffering servant of Isaiah 53:5: "with his stripes we are healed."

If we consider carefully the context of Isaiah 53:5 and 1 Peter 2:24, the meaning of "healed" may mean either physical or spiritual healing. But despite the healing of our wounds finding its ultimate fulfilment at the resurrection, the context seems to refer primarily to spiritual healing. Isaiah 53:5 reads, "But he was wounded for *our transgressions*; he was crushed for *our iniquities*; upon him was the chastisement that brought us peace, and with his stripes we are healed" (emphasis mine). Similarly, Peter wrote, "He himself bore *our sins* in his body on the tree, that we might *die to sin and live to righteousness. By his wounds you have been healed*" (emphasis mine). Jesus heals us from our sin so that we might live to righteousness. If we were to take Peter's words "By his wounds you have been healed" to mean literal physical healing, then it would be difficult to conceive why many Christians suffer from disease and sickness. Faithful Christians still endure physical suffering! Therefore, considering the context, it is reasonable to think of healing first in terms of spiritual healing from sin and its consequences, and ultimately as physical healing at the resurrection, when we will be given eternal resurrected bodies.

The apostle expands on his thought in 1 Peter 3:18, 22. In verse 18 he writes, "For Christ also suffered once for sins, the righteous for the unrighteous, that he might bring us to God, being put to death in the flesh but made alive in the spirit." In this verse we observe the emphasis on Jesus suffering *for* our sins. Yet again we note the reference to the suffering servant of Isaiah 53:11–12. "The righteous for the unrighteous" of course expresses penal substitution. The conjunction "that" points us to the purpose for which Christ suffered for the unrighteous, that is, "*that* he might bring us to God." Through Jesus's sacrificial death we are reconciled to God our Father; it is Christ who accomplishes our reconciliation.

In verse 22, Peter offers a description of Jesus's heavenly position: "who has gone into heaven and is at the right hand of God, with angels, authorities, and powers having been subjected to him." Jesus is said to be seated at the right hand of God, another reference to Psalm 110. Like other New Testament authors, Peter too uses the terms "authorities and powers" to indicate the rulers of the spirit world. This might include human rulers on earth as well. Therefore, all angels, authorities and powers have been subjected to Jesus Christ.

Having explored the atonement in numerous key passages in the Bible, we find a harmony between the penal substitution and Christus Victor theories that we must appreciate when talking about the atonement. There is a togetherness of these two views in Scripture. Many churches and theologians today neglect one of these views for the sake of the other, creating what I believe is a distorted theology of atonement.

However, Christian theology has not always emphasized one part of the atonement over another. In the next chapter I will show that over the centuries Christian theology has embraced both penal substitution and Christus Victor in the understanding of atonement.

3

Atonement in Christian Theology

Before we look at the exciting topic of the atonement in Christian theology I must make it clear that all theology must be submitted to Scripture . . . always! However, we all interpret Scripture differently because of our various life experiences, backgrounds and cultural contexts; therefore, theology must always be done in community – that is, we know God and study his ways together. Even though we may disagree on some points of theology with many of the great people of faith, the church fathers and the theologians in the history of the church, there is still much we can learn from them. My aim in this chapter is to offer an overview, without becoming too detailed.

As we shall see, penal substitution and Christus Victor have been very much present in the major periods of Christian history and in many of the great Christian thinkers. What is of special interest for our purposes, though, is that the development of atonement theology in church history started with the church fathers, many of whom were African – notably Athanasius and Augustine (whom we will look at below), and also Tertullian and Origen.

Church Fathers

The early church suffered intense persecution at the hands of the pagan Roman Empire. The world of suffering and persecution in which they lived was understandably interpreted within a spiritual-warfare context, with many Christians seeing it as a struggle between the cross and the sword, between God and the evil forces of darkness. Such a context caused theologians of this era to think of the atonement in terms of Christus Victor, and yet we will see that the understanding of a substitutionary atonement was evident as well.

Ignatius of Antioch, a disciple of the apostle John who lived around 50–117, was one of the first church fathers. Apparently he wrote letters while on his way from Antioch to Rome to face martyrdom. In these letters one can sense Ignatius's imminent martyrdom and his preparation for an agonizing death, and how it shapes his understanding of the atonement. Thinking about his own suffering to come, he reminds himself and his readers that our Saviour Jesus Christ suffered for our sins, and that the Father raised him up again. He also focuses on the cross which becomes a victory through Jesus's resurrection and the ground by which salvation is secured.[1] You can see both substitutionary atonement and Christus Victor in his thinking, and you can also feel his sense of hope in the resurrection and victory despite his approaching death.

Another early church father, Justin Martyr (c.103–165), was both a philosopher and an apologist. He wanted to win unbelievers over to Christianity, and did this by finding connections between the gospel and the intellectual concepts and culture of his audience, without compromising the Christian message. In an important work, Justin recorded a dialogue with a learned Jew, Trypho. Knowing that Trypho was Jewish, Justin focused his discussions with him on the foreshadowing of the cross in the Old Testament.

In one brilliant example of this, Justin reminds Trypho about the Passover lamb, whose blood on the doorposts and lintels delivered the Israelites from death and then out of Egypt. In many ways this Passover lamb was substitutionary as well as a sacrifice, and in the end it enabled victory over the Egyptians. Justin then compares Christ to this Passover lamb, Christ being the new Passover lamb who was sacrificed.[2]

Irenaeus of Lyons (c.115–202), who was somewhat different from Justin, had a special interest in the saving work of Christ. He developed the history of salvation, the idea of humanity fallen in Adam being restarted by Christ, whereby a new humankind, a new creation, would find its fulfilment in Jesus. For there to be this new creation, Irenaeus said that Christ had to be incarnated and take part in human nature.

In Irenaeus's work *Against Heresies* he understood that through Adam's disobedience, all humanity came under Satan's rule and that Jesus's death was a victory over sin, death and the devil. Irenaeus was the first of the early church fathers to emphasize the consequences of Adam's sin and that each individual person has participated in Adam's disobedience. He taught that Jesus is the

---

1. Ignatius, "Epistle to the Smyrneans" 7, in *The Apostolic Fathers with Justin Martyr and Irenaeus*, vol. 1 of *The Ante-Nicene Fathers*, ed. A. Roberts and J. Donaldson (New York: Cosimo Classics, 2007), 87–89.

2. Justin Martyr, "Dialogue with Trypho the Jew" 111, in Roberts and Donaldson, *Apostolic Fathers*, 244–51.

second Adam, having undone the evils brought by the first Adam and put right every part of the disobedience of Adam and his offspring, thereby restoring communion with God. For Irenaeus, the atonement touches the very fabric of human life.

The prolific early church theologian Athanasius wrote in section 4 of his *On the Incarnation* that Jesus Christ the Word came down to us because our transgressions cried out to him, that he might in his love for us appear and help us. He then talked about humanity's depravity and how humankind "turned from the contemplation of God to the evil of their own devising"[3] and so "came inevitably under the law of death."[4] Thus, humanity found themselves becoming progressively corrupt, and death ruled over them as their transgressions against the commandments of God made them "turn back again according to their nature."[5]

J. N. D. Kelly tells us that Athanasius's theology of salvation was primarily about Christ who, by becoming man, restored the divine image in us, together with the conviction that his death was necessary to release us from the curse of sin, and that he offered himself in sacrifice for us. Jesus's sacrifice on our behalf was therefore understood in terms of penal substitution.[6]

In another work, Athanasius provides us with an outstanding discussion alluding to Christus Victor, proclaiming that all things were delivered to Christ, and that while he was made to be man, all things were set right and perfected. Instead of a curse, the earth receives a blessing. "Paradise was opened to the robber, Hades cowered, the tombs were opened and the dead raised." Athanasius focused on the substitutionary theme when he wrote, "For he bore the indignation which lay upon us."[7] But perhaps Athanasius's strongest expression of penal substitution is found in his *Orations against the Arians*, where he says, "Formerly the world, as guilty, was under judgement from the Law; but now the Word has taken on himself the judgement, and

3. Athanasius, *On the Incarnation*, Section 4, in Series 2, vol. 4 of *The Nicene and Post-Nicene Fathers*, eds. Philip Schaff and Henry Wace, 14 vols. (repr.; Grand Rapids: Eerdmans, 1978).

4. Athanasius, *On the Incarnation*, Section 4.

5. Athanasius, *On the Incarnation*, Section 4.

6. J. N. D. Kelly, *Early Christian Doctrines*, 4th ed. (London: Adam & Charles Black, 1968), 377.

7. Athanasius, *In Illud Omnia: on Luke 10:22 (Matthew 11:27)*, Section 2, in Series 2, vol. 4 of *The Nicene and Post-Nicene Fathers*, eds. Philip Schaff and Henry Wace, 14 vols. (repr.; Grand Rapids, MI: Eerdmans, 1978).

having suffered in the body for all, has bestowed salvation to all."[8] Athanasius positioned penal substitution at the very heart of his theology, as essential to the purpose of the incarnation as well as to the restoration of humanity and creation.

John Chrysostom (*c*.349–407), called the "silver-tongue" because of his oratory eloquence, did not purpose to develop a theology of the atonement as did Athanasius. However, in his *Homilies on 2 Corinthians* 11.6, he tells the story of a king who sympathizes with a condemned robber to the extent of giving his own son to receive the guilt and the death penalty in the criminal's stead. Over and above this sacrifice, the king exalts the criminal to great dignity. Chrysostom used this story to show how God allowed his Son to suffer as a condemned sinner, though he was perfect and sinless, so that he might deliver us from the penalty of sin and offer us salvation. He understood humankind as having been condemned to death by God, and yet Jesus substituted himself in our place. Our guilt and death were transferred to Christ; and his sacrifice was of such surpassing worth that it was sufficient to save humanity.

The Latin church father Hilary of Poitiers (*c*.300–368) associated satisfaction with sacrifice and understood the cross of Christ as an act of compensation to God on our behalf. We see this in Hilary's *Treatise on the Psalms* 53, where he emphasizes that Jesus sacrificed himself freely and offered himself voluntarily as a victim to God the Father, "in order that by means of a voluntary victim the curse which attended the discontinuance of the regular victim might be removed."[9] Hilary's theology shows us that everyone who has broken the law of God is under his curse, and that the rituals and sacrifices in the Old Testament were necessary to escape God's punishment of death. In his writings, Hilary focused on Jesus's sacrifice while stressing the voluntary nature of his death and what it has achieved. Christ's death destroyed the sentence of death which was due to us and reunited us to God. The sacrificial theme is also prominent in Hilary's atonement theology which ultimately points towards the Christus Victor theme – that is, in Christ's sacrifice there is victory over death.

Following on from this idea of a curse, the teaching of Ambrose of Milan (*c*.339–397) rests on the theology of penal substitution. The curse that was on fallen humanity was transferred to Jesus Christ, and he died in our stead to satisfy God's justice.

---

8. Athanasius, *Orations against the Arians*, in Series 2, vol. 4 of *The Nicene and Post-Nicene Fathers*, eds. Philip Schaff and Henry Wace, 14 vols. (repr.; Grand Rapids: Eerdmans, 1975).

9. Hilary of Poitiers, *Homily on Psalm 53,* Series 2, vol.9 of *The Nicene and Post-Nicene Fathers*, eds. Philip Schaff and Henry Wace, 14 vols. (repr.; Grand Rapids, MI: Eerdmans, 1975).

The man who was perhaps most inspired and influenced by Ambrose was Augustine (354–430) from North Africa: he too continued the theme of curse in his *Disputation against Fortunatus the Manichaean* 14.4, proclaiming,

> The apostle boldly says of Christ, "He was made a curse for us"; for he could also venture to say, "He died for all." "He died," and "He was cursed," are the same. Death is the effect of the curse; and all sin is cursed, whether it means the action which merits punishment, or the punishment which follows. Christ, though guiltless, took our punishment, that he might cancel our guilt, and do away with our punishment.[10]

In section 6 of the same work, Augustine develops this thought: "And as he died in the flesh which he took in bearing our punishment . . . he was cursed for our offences, in the death which he suffered in bearing our punishment."[11] Further, in *On the Trinity* he states, "As our death is the punishment of sin, so his death was made a sacrifice for sin."[12]

The church fathers thus had a strong understanding of Jesus's atoning work on the cross, an understanding that often included both penal substitution and Christus Victor. Next, we shall see what the atonement looked like for the Scholastics, the churchmen who lived during the Middle Ages.

Scholastics

Medieval architecture, notably its cathedrals, gives evidence of a continuing sense of a demonic presence. As an architect, I love visiting grand buildings, and so when I had the opportunity I visited Paris and saw Notre-Dame Cathedral as well as the cathedral in Cologne. It is difficult to ignore the gargoyles that decorate such cathedrals. Often these demonic figures are portrayed as having been conquered. The cathedral was a place of worship, but it was also, back in its early days, a common place for exorcisms and rituals where people could purify themselves and fend off demonic forces. Though these devils were supposedly conquered, the fear of the demonic remained in the church and among Christians during the medieval period, not to mention the obsession

---

10. Augustine, *Acts Or Disputation Against Fortunatus The Manichaean,* 14:4, Series 1, vol. 4 of *The Nicene and Post-Nicene Fathers,* eds. Philip Schaff and Henry Wace, 14 vols. (repr.; Grand Rapids: Eerdmans, 1975).

11. Augustine, *Acts Or Disputation Against Fortunatus The Manichaean,* 14:6.

12. Augustine, "On the Holy Trinity" 4.12, Series 1, vol. 3 of *The Nicene and Post-Nicene Fathers,* eds. Philip Schaff and Henry Wace, 14 vols. (repr.; Grand Rapids, MI: Eerdmans, 1975).

with the persecution of witches and heretics. As we shall see in part 2 of this book, a similar fear exists in Africa even today.

The first major theologian to come on the scene during this time was Anselm of Canterbury (1033–1109). He wrote *Cur Deus Homo*, a Latin title which means "Why God Became Human." In this work, Anselm sought, by reason alone, to persuade those who do not have faith in the Trinity and to prove the existence of God independently from the authority of Scripture. *Cur Deus Homo* was also the first treatise to make a serious attempt at rationalizing the atonement, bringing an aspect of substitution to the forefront of atonement theology. It was perhaps one of the most influential works on the atonement in the Western church.

The context of Anselm's atonement theology in *Cur Deus Homo* was feudalism, given that feudal law dominated life, with penalties and punishments meted out for offences committed. It is apparent that Anselm drew on these ideas from his own context in his work on the atonement.

For example, the honour of God which Anselm explores in *Cur Deus Homo* makes sense only within the context of honour in the empire, and satisfaction is a means of restoring the honour and so preserving the order of the empire. Jesus, having become a man, thus preserved God's honour and brought about restoration to the universe. As Reeves explains:

> The concept of honour is a feudal concept; God has been wronged. Sin costs more than Creation; God himself is worth more than creation. Christ, the God-man, has given himself [in the] priceless gift of his own death. Once the God-man has done that, then God would have to reward the God-man because the God-man did not have to offer himself up but he chose to live the perfect life and went beyond that and therefore God must justly reward him.[13]

Anselm understood that human sin and disobedience disrupted the "ordered relationship of beauty and harmony." The consequence was disharmony and disorder. However, it was the death of Jesus, the God-man – which was not required but was freely given to satisfy God's honour – that restored order. In *Cur Deus Homo*, Anselm describes sin as follows: "He who

---

13. Michael Reeves, "Introducing Anselm," online lecture, 2011, accessed 22 February 2011, http://www.theologynetwork.org/historical-theology/getting-stuck-in/introducing----anselm-of-canterbury.htm.

does not render this honour which is due to God, robs God of his own and dishonours him; and this is sin."[14]

It was not that God's wrath had to be appeased, but rather his honour had to be restored, according to Anselm. God is the sovereign ruler of the universe and his honour must not be trampled upon. For Anselm, Christ was not understood as a substitute bearing our punishment; instead Jesus offered his life to God as an offering of greater worth than God could justly demand, and in this God's honour was satisfied. This is the meaning of satisfaction. The debt was infinite, and none other than an infinite being was able to satisfy it, and yet only a human being could bring about compensation. The only solution was that God must become man – which is the answer to *Cur Deus Homo*, "Why God Became Human." Jesus submitted his life unto death, and thus acquired merit of infinite value, which covers the infinite guilt of human sin, thereby achieving satisfaction.

Some theologians today argue that Anselm prepared the way in atonement theology for a "cosmic child abuse" theology, a son being punished by a wrathful father for someone else's sin. In *Cur Deus Homo* 1.8–9, Anselm rejects the notion that Jesus's suffering was compelled by the Father. He says that the "Son wished to die for the salvation of the world."[15] Furthermore, Anselm also pointed to the Christus Victor theme when he wrote,

> But God demanded that man should conquer the devil, so that he who had offended by sin should atone by holiness. As God owed nothing to the devil but punishment, so man must only make amends by conquering the devil as man had already been conquered by him. But whatever was demanded of man, he owed to God and not to the devil.[16]

Anselm never rejected the idea of humanity having sold itself into the devil's bondage, and he had no problem with Christ's death being a ransom for humanity's sin which rescued people from the devil. Anselm did, however, reject the idea of a payment made to Satan. It is reasonable, I think, to say that Anselm taught a satisfaction theory together with the Christus Victor theme.

---

14. Anselm, *Cur Deus Homo* 1.11, in *Proslogium; Monologium; An Appendix in Behalf of the Fool by Gaunilon; and Cur Deus Homo*, 1099, trans. by Sidney Norton Deane (Chicago: Open Court Publishing, 1926), Christian Classics Ethereal Library, accessed 1 May 2011, http://www.ccel.org/ccel/anselm/basic_works.html.

15. Anselm, *Cur Deus Homo* 1.10.

16. Anselm, *Cur Deus Homo* 2.19.

The prominent philosopher and theologian Peter Abelard (1079–1142) lived in Paris in the shadow of Notre-Dame. While Abelard was a genius of Christian theology and philosophy, his life was marked by tragedy. In his early years he supported himself by tutoring Héloïse, the daughter of an important citizen of Paris. The two fell in love, which resulted in a pregnancy, and although the child would be illegitimate they married secretly. Unfortunately for Abelard, Héloïse's uncle found out, and in fury had him castrated.

Abelard explains in his *Exposition of Romans* 3.26 that our redemption is the highest love shown by the passion of Christ which liberates us from slavery to sin and "wins for us the true liberty of the sons of God, so that we may fulfil all things from love rather than from fear." Abelard did not reject Anselm's "satisfaction" idea entirely, for a notion of penal substitution is evident in his writings as well. For Abelard said of Christ, "He suffered truly for your salvation, on your behalf, of his own free will, and by his suffering he cures all sickness and removes all suffering."[17] He explained how this was achieved when he wrote,

> First, because the faults for which he died were ours, and we committed the sins for which he bore the punishment; secondly, that by dying he might remove our sins, that is, the punishment of our sins, introducing us into paradise at the price of his own death, and might, by the display of grace such that he himself said, "Greater love hath no man," draw our minds away from the will to sin and enkindle in them the highest love of himself.[18]

Nevertheless, the shape of Abelard's atonement theology took on what is often called "moral influence theology" and received severe criticism, especially from Bernard of Clairvaux, who wrote to Pope Innocent III hoping to condemn Abelard. Bernard believed that Abelard's atonement theology had Pelagian tendencies and that it made the cross merely into an example of Christ's love.

We move on to one of the greatest theologians of the church, Thomas Aquinas (1225–1274), sometimes called "the Prince of European Scholasticism." He stands alongside Augustine in intellectual ability and influence.

---

17. Peter Abelard, *The Letters of Héloïse and Abelard* (Harmondsworth: Penguin, 1974).

18. Peter Abelard, exposition of Romans 4:25, quoted in Larry Siekawitch, "The Evolution of the Doctrine of the Atonement in the Medieval Church: Anselm, Abelard and Aquinas," *McMaster Journal of Theology and Ministry* 9 (2007–2008): 3–30; see also Peter Abelard, exposition of Romans 4:25; 8:3, quoted in H. D. McDonald, *The Atonement of the Death of Christ: In Faith, Revelation, and History* (Grand Rapids: Baker, 1985), 177; and Ian J. Shaw and Brian H. Edwards, *The Divine Substitute: The Atonement in the Bible and History* (Leominster: Day One Publications, 2006), 72.

At the very core of Aquinas's understanding of the atonement was Jesus's death as a substitutionary sacrifice which dealt with the penalty of sin that was owed to God and therefore satisfied his justice. The cross provides redemption for sinners from punishment and slavery to sin.

For Aquinas, this redemption was so arranged to reveal the love and *also* the justice of God. In Aquinas's major work, *Summa Theologica* ("Summary of Theology"), he wrote that it was by means of Christ's passion that he "made satisfaction for the sin of the human race." It was because of Christ's justice and mercy that humanity was set free, because humankind of their own accord were incapable of making satisfaction for the sin of all humanity.[19]

Our debt was due by us, for we have sinned against God, yet he paid it himself by giving his own Son as a propitiation.[20] Christ's work, therefore, paid the ransom price and made satisfaction. Although Christ made the offering in his human nature, being God his passion was of infinite worth and therefore made "a superabundant atonement for the sins of the human race."[21] Aquinas proclaimed that "when sufficient satisfaction has been paid then the debt of punishment is abolished."[22]

Aquinas supposed that humanity was held in bondage on account of sin in two ways. First, Satan overcame humanity by provoking them to sin, and therefore humanity became subject to Satan's bondage. Second, humanity are held in bondage by God's justice, and so they are accountable for the payment of a debt of punishment. However, Christ's sufficient and superabundant atonement for sin frees humanity from their obligations.[23]

So far, Aquinas's understanding of the atonement is strong. However, it weakens when he begins to emphasize the sacrament of penance in appropriating the atonement. Such penance includes contrition, confession, faith, love, baptism and other acts of absolution. These apparently "unite people to the atonement of Christ and become a necessary part of it."[24] Presumably, the atonement is superabundant only if you do penance! It is by means of penance that one is able to enjoy the benefits of the atonement, according to Aquinas. Christ's death on the cross must first be applied in our lives before it is effective.

---

19. Thomas Aquinas, *Summa Theologica*, trans. by the Fathers of the English Dominican Province (New York: Benziger Bros., 1947), Q.46, A.3.

20. Aquinas, *Summa Theologica*, Q.47, A.3.

21. Aquinas, Q.48, A.3.

22. Aquinas, Q.49, A.3.

23. Aquinas, Q.48, A.4.

24. Gregg R. Allison, *Historical Theology: An Introduction to Christian Doctrine* (Grand Rapids: Zondervan, 2011), 398; Siekawitch, "Doctrine of the Atonement," 24.

According to this view, both Christ's work and the sacraments are needed for a full legal satisfaction. In other words, acts of repentance or penance fill up what is lacking in Christ's satisfaction. It is difficult to appreciate Aquinas's view of atonement when he implies that "human cooperation with the work of Christ is necessary" in appropriating the atonement![25] I don't doubt that this is true in terms of faith and repentance, but regarding other acts of penance it seems to me to be contrary to Aquinas's understanding of a "superabundant" atonement; the idea that we need to "top it up" with penance is dubious. Scripture makes it clear that Jesus's atonement made on the cross is altogether adequate and infinitely sufficient, without our needing to add to it.

Reformers

The atonement theology found in the works of the Reformers is somewhat similar to Anselm's theology, but with an important difference. Anselm's satisfaction theory highlighted the "honour of God"; the Reformers, however, emphasized the "justice of God." The Reformers stressed the idea of *penalty* in substitutionary atonement, and yet Christ the Victor also dominated their thinking. I shall begin by exploring Martin Luther's atonement theology, and then move on to John Calvin.

The method of theology used by Luther was quite different from that of the church fathers. For him, Christ was central, and Luther had a profound understanding of the fall, sin, the depravity of humanity and the bondage of the human will.

Luther, a sixteenth-century monk and professor of theology, experienced a prolonged struggle with what he called his *Anfechtung*, meaning "challenge." He would stretch himself to the limit to seek to relieve himself from guilt and condemnation. He attempted to satisfy God in prayer, vigils, fasting and good works, but all to no avail. This is similar to Aquinas's idea of penance in appropriating the atonement.

Responding to Luther's despair, his confessor, Staupitz, directed him to the cross, "the wounds of the sweet saviour." The very heart of Luther's struggle was a pursuit of the assurance of his salvation. Eventually, Luther began to see the cross of Christ as the place of Satan's defeat and the basis for "justification by faith alone." If you read Luther's works, you soon notice how he sees the atonement as both a penal substitution and a victory over Satan. These became crucial for Luther's understanding of atonement. Luther viewed

---

25. Allison, *Historical Theology*, 398.

Christ's satisfaction as perfect and sufficient; there was no need for additional satisfaction on the part of human beings.

Of course, satisfaction in Luther's day was related to the medieval sacrament of penance. And while Anselm taught that God either inflicted a penalty or provided satisfaction, Luther, on the other hand, argued that God did both: that Christ in his death "bears all the sins of all men in his body" and bearing our penalty makes "satisfaction for them with his own blood." Punishment is paid and God's justice is satisfied![26] Nevertheless, Luther wished to have the satisfaction theory abolished from Christian theology, and felt that it belonged to the legal profession. For him, the idea of satisfaction was so much a part of the system of penance that he despised it, and believed that it obscured the gospel.

For this reason, Luther says that satisfaction alone is "too weak" a description for Christ's atoning work on the cross. His understanding of atonement theology, and in fact all his theology, is shaped by the contrast of the "theology of glory" and the "theology of the cross."[27] For Luther, the cross alone is our theology.

The cross was first "God's attack on human sin" and second salvation from sin. But this "attack" on sin was a strange attack, for Christ suffered and died at the hand of humanity. It was God's "alien work." Forde explains that the cross of Christ does not call for a passive response, but it "draws us into itself so that we become participants in the story. . . . Just as Jesus was crucified so we also are crucified with him. The cross makes us part of its story."[28]

Luther's central idea in his atonement theology comes together in his exposition of Galatians, especially Galatians 3:13. In this exposition, he presents both Christ's victory and his work of atonement. Luther taught that Christ secured redemption while "facing death, while agonizing under the wrath of a holy God opposed to sinful man." This was the means by which Christ conquered the devil, death and sin.[29] For "Christ's righteousness is unconquerable. Sin is defeated and righteousness triumphs and reigns forever.

---

26. Martin Luther, *Luther's Works*, eds. J. Pelikan and H. T. Lehmann (Philadelphia: Fortress, 1955–1974), 26:277.

27. Luther's *Heidelberg Disputation*, Theses 19–21, in Gerhard O. Forde, *On Being a Theologian of the Cross: Reflections on Luther's Heidelberg Disputation, 1518* (Grand Rapids: Eerdmans, 1997).

28. Forde, *Theologian of the Cross*, 1, 7, 12.

29. Annette Gundrum Aubert, "Luther, Melanchthon, and Chemnitz: The Doctrine of the Atonement with Special Reference to Gustaf Aulén's Christus Victor" (Master's thesis, Westminster Theological Seminary, 2002), 59. Available at www.tren.com.

In the same manner death was defeated. . . . Sin, death, the wrath of God, hell, the devil are mortified in Christ."[30]

Another important Reformer was John Calvin of Geneva (1509–1564). He is arguably one of the church's greatest theologians, along with Augustine and Aquinas. He also shared Luther's conviction that the atonement was at the very centre of Christian theology. It is noteworthy that Calvin's theology of atonement was rooted in a passionate pastoral concern. He provides a stunning demonstration in the penal substitutionary atonement of God's fury against sin set against his intense love for the sinner.

In Calvin's *Institutes of Christian Religion*, he explains that through his suffering Jesus overcame death, "that he might subject the weakness of the one to death as an expiation of sin, and by the power of the other, maintaining a struggle with death, might gain us the victory."[31] Christ therefore engaged "with the powers of hell and the horrors of eternal death"[32] in this struggle. Calvin says that humanity were under the curse of eternal death and thus "excluded from all hope of salvation";[33] certainly they were held captive to sin and enslaved by the devil. But Jesus Christ intervened! Calvin proclaims that by Christ's enduring the curse, Jesus "annihilated all its force,"[34] and referring to the writings of the apostle Paul Calvin tells us that Christ triumphed upon the cross, the symbol of humiliation, and exchanged it for "a triumphal chariot" in which he defeated the principalities and powers. But Calvin also makes it clear that in Christ's rising again, Jesus "became victorious over death, so the victory of our faith consists only in his resurrection."[35] Further, by becoming man, Christ presented "our flesh as the price of satisfaction to the just judgement of God, and in the same flesh paid the penalty which we had incurred."[36]

And so, in a time of crippling fear, guilt and anxiety, the Reformers sought to find a way back to the origins of the Christian gospel, where free grace and assurance of salvation could be known once again.

---

30. Luther on Galatians 3:13, in Martin Luther, *Commentary on Galatians* (Logos ed.; Dallas: Word Incorporated, 1996).

31. John Calvin, *Institutes of the Christian Religion*. Trans. by H. Beveridge (Peabody: Hendrickson Publishers, 2008), 2.12.3, 299.

32. John Calvin, *Institutes of the Christian Religion*, 2.16.10, 331.

33. John Calvin, *Institutes of the Christian Religion*, 2.16.2, 325.

34. John Calvin, *Institutes of the Christian Religion*, 2.16.6, 329.

35. John Calvin, *Institutes of the Christian Religion*, 2.16.13, 334.

36. John Calvin, *Institutes of the Christian Religion*, 2.12.3, 299.

Post-Reformation

The theologians of the Post-Reformation period usually had an anti-supernatural worldview. Yet even those Reformed theologians who believed in the supernatural in some sense, such as François Turrettini, Charles Hodge and Louis Berkhof, did not explore seriously the theme of Christ conquering the devil.

Turrettini of Geneva (1623–1687; also known as Francis Turretin) was a theologian who overlapped the Reformation and Post-Reformation eras. He taught penal substitutionary atonement, proclaiming our liberation from guilt while preserving God's justice. He said that Christ, in his life and death, had made satisfaction, which God accepted, and therefore God could forgive us our sins. Therefore, "justice is exercised against sin, and mercy towards the sinner; an atonement is made to the divine justice by a surety, and God mercifully pardons us," said Turrettini.[37]

Turrettini's atonement theology was also expressed in the theology of the towering theologian John Owen (1616–1683). Owen's atonement theology, however, was focused primarily against the idea of universal redemption. Famous among Puritan thinkers, Owen is possibly the greatest of English theologians.

According to Owen, the punishment that Jesus bore in his death was the exact equivalent of the sins and punishment deserved by all believers. He later made it clear "that Christ died for all in respect of the sufficiency of the ransom he paid, but not in respect of the efficacy of its application."[38] However, Owen certainly believed that the invitation to accept the gospel is universal because it is addressed to every person, and all who come to Christ will be received by him.

While John Owen was the greatest of English theologians, Jonathan Edwards (1703–1758) was perhaps the greatest American theologian. Edwards's preaching of the gospel of Christ's satisfaction for sin was instrumental in the 1734–35 and 1740–41 revivals. In his sermons he would "set the love of God firmly alongside the justice of God as the reason for the atonement."[39] Edwards

---

37. Francis Turretin, "The Necessity of the Atonement," chapter 1 of *The Atonement of Christ*, trans. J. R. Wilson, A Puritan's Mind, accessed 2 May 2011, https://www.apuritansmind.com/puritan-favorites/francis-turretin/the-necessity-of-the-atonement/.

38. John Owen, *The Death of Death in the Death of Christ* (Edinburgh: The Banner of Truth Trust, 1959), 168, 184.

39. Shaw and Edwards, *Divine Substitute*, 100. See Jonathan Edwards's sermon "Sinners in the Hands of an Angry God," 8 July 1741, Christian Classics Ethereal Library, accessed 1 June 2014, https://www.ccel.org/ccel/edwards/sermons.sinners.html.

taught that Christ's passion revealed the fullness of his love for humankind and the honour and love of the majesty of God. Therefore, in light of God's holiness and majesty, "there is no escape from the penalty of sin which has insulted God. The terrible reality of man's doom is therefore imminent, unless a satisfaction of eternal worth can be found to counterbalance the divine decree."[40]

Edwards emphasized the infinite worth of Christ's work, which met the infinite penalty for our sin. He explained that satisfaction and merit "both consist in paying a valuable price, a price of infinite value: but only that price, as it respects a debt to be paid, is called *satisfaction*; and as it respects a positive good to be obtained, is called *merit*."[41]

Some years later, the orthodox Calvinism of the Western Confession was challenged as liberal theology advanced. It was during these troubling times that Charles Hodge (1797–1878), in his *Systematic Theology*, provided a defence of orthodoxy, including the traditional view of penal substitution. He felt that it was appropriate to use legal language when talking of the atonement, because justice is a vital feature of God's nature. Speaking of Christ, Hodge said that his work satisfies the demands of the law. Hodge developed his atonement theology in ways very similar to Edwards.

Like Hodge, B. B. Warfield (1851–1921), a Princeton theologian, was also concerned about Christian orthodoxy and the traditional view of penal substitution. He stated that "the doctrine of substitutive atonement . . . is, after all, the very heart of the gospel."[42] Like the theologians before him, Warfield sought to highlight the love of God in the atonement. The love of God is the basis of the atonement. Expositing John 3:16, he comments, "God's love of the world is shown by his saving so great a multitude as he does save out of the world."[43] He explained that the primary intention of salvation "is to convey some conception of the immeasurable greatness of the love of God. The method it employs to do this is to declare the love of God for the world so great that he gave his Son to save it."[44] For Warfield, this salvation was purchased and secured

---

40. McDonald, *Atonement of the Death of Christ*, 298.

41. Jonathan Edwards, "History of Redemption," in vol. 2 of *The Works of Jonathan Edwards* (1773; Peabody: Hendrickson, 1993), 574.

42. B. B. Warfield, *The Person and Work of Christ*, ed. S. G. Craig (Philadelphia: Presbyterian & Reformed, 1950), 377.

43. B. B. Warfield, *The Saviour of the World* (Edinburgh: The Banner of Truth Trust, 1916), 114.

44. Warfield, *Saviour of the World*, 115.

"through a satisfaction that could be rendered only through substitutionary sacrifice and blood-brought redemption."[45]

The theology of Jonathan Edwards lived on in Louis Berkhof (1873–1957) of the Calvin Theological Seminary. McDonald explains how Berkhof saw the atonement as an absolute necessity, because rebellion cannot simply be disregarded in light of God's infinite majesty and perfections. Sin must be punished.[46] With respect to God's love in the atonement, Berkhof cautioned against representing a "sympathetic love of Christ for sinners," offering himself in the sinner's stead, pacifying an angry God. Berkhof felt that this was all wrong and that it "presupposes a schism in the Trinitarian life of God."[47] Rather, he said,

> the good pleasure of God to save sinners by a substitutionary atonement was founded in the love and justice of God. It was the love of God that provided a way of escape for lost sinners, John 3:16. And it was the justice of God which required that this way should be of such a nature as to meet the demands of the law.[48]

Therefore, the atonement cannot be explained on the basis of God's love alone, and yet it was "the good pleasure of God to save sinners by a substitutionary atonement."[49]

Following closely behind Berkhof was Anthony Hoekema (1913–1988), who was in agreement with him. Hoekema explained that God is full of wrath against sin. But at the same time, "God has so richly shown his love to us that he gave his Son for us, so that through the shedding of Christ's blood the Father's wrath against our sin could be removed." Therefore, it is through Christ's substitutionary sacrifice that God's wrath against our sin is turned aside, as Jesus bore his wrath in our stead.[50]

Focusing our attention again on British theologians, London preacher Charles H. Spurgeon (1834–1892), sometimes called the "Prince of Preachers," was deeply concerned about the lack of preaching of the cross in many sermons. He made it clear that Christ took our sins upon himself and suffered for them

---

45. John Murray, *Redemption: Accomplished and Applied* (Edinburgh: The Banner of Truth Trust, 1955), 56, 62.

46. McDonald, *Atonement of the Death of Christ*, 310; Louis Berkhof, *Systematic Theology* (Grand Rapids: Eerdmans, 1996), 371.

47. Berkhof, *Systematic Theology*, 367.

48. Berkhof, 368.

49. Berkhof, 363, 367–68.

50. Anthony A. Hoekema, *Saved from Grace* (Grand Rapids: Eerdmans, 1989), 158, 174.

on the cross, and that in this way our debt was paid and our transgressions removed by his blood for ever. He explained further that it is "because God has condemned sin in the flesh of Jesus Christ [that] he will no more condemn us – we are henceforth free – that the righteousness of the Law may be fulfilled in us."[51]

Spurgeon's cause for concern was a rising tide of criticism about the traditional view of atonement, and this did not abate. In fact, at the dawn of the twentieth century some theologians sought to boldly defend substitutionary atonement, most notably the Scottish theologian James Denney (1856–1917). He argued that the atonement was central to the New Testament and that there was no gospel without it. Denney believed that the atonement was "God's response to a profound problem: 'Sin in me is as deep as my being.'" Denney was emphatic that "Christ, by God's appointment, dies the sinner's death. The doom falls upon him, and is exhausted there." For in redeeming us, Christ became a curse for us, "that we might become the righteousness of God in him."[52]

Another great London preacher, Dr. Martyn Lloyd-Jones (1899–1981) of Westminster Chapel, saw the atonement as the most marvellous and magnificent event in all of history. Commenting on Romans 3:20 – 4:2, he described ransoming as redemption. God ransoms us from our sins by means of a propitiatory sacrifice. Therefore, the remission of sin can be dealt with only by means of shedding blood and thus appeasing the wrath of God.[53] In his writings, Lloyd-Jones makes it clear that God offers propitiation from within himself, to satisfy and appease his *own* wrath. The propitiation is not provided by another person, but by himself.

The harmony of the penal substitution and Christus Victor themes is seen most strikingly in the following words he wrote:

> So you see that our Lord by his work, and especially his work upon the cross, in addition to bearing the penalty and punishment of our sins as our substitute, was also destroying the works of the devil, he was delivering us from the bondage and the dominion of

---

51. Charles H. Spurgeon, "Sorrow at the Cross Turned into Joy," Sermon no. 1442, 5, 3 November 1878, Spurgeon Gems, accessed 4 June 2011, https://www.spurgeongems.org/sermon/chs1442.pdf.

52. James Denney, *Studies in Theology: Lectures Delivered in Chicago Theological Seminary*, 3rd ed. (London: Hodder & Stoughton, 1895), 111, 115.

53. Martyn Lloyd-Jones, *Romans: An Exposition of Chapters 3.20 – 4.25 – Atonement and Justification* (Edinburgh: The Banner of Truth Trust, 1970), 81, 89; Martyn Lloyd-Jones, *God the Father, God the Son*, vol. 1 of *Great Doctrines of the Bible* (Wheaton: Crossway, 2003), 322.

the devil, and was also delivering us from the territory of death. We are no longer dead in trespasses and sins; we do not belong to the realm of death, we are alive unto God. And likewise he has delivered us from the tyranny and thraldom and power of sin.[54]

The Anglican theologian J. I. Packer was profoundly influenced by Lloyd-Jones, and he too courageously defended penal substitution against liberals and some evangelicals who dismissed it as offensive and outdated. During his studies in Oxford, Packer came across the Puritan John Owen. Owen had considerable impact upon Packer's theology, notably in his atonement theology. Packer argued that the atonement in penal substitutionary terms was planned by all members of the Trinity. For him, the right view of the atonement is of utmost importance, because it is bound up in the character of God. The meaning of Christianity is at stake if an incorrect view of the atonement is held, Packer believed.[55]

In his writings, Packer articulated the atonement as Christ taking the place of sinners who are exposed to God's divine judgement, and in so doing laying down his life as a sacrifice, undergoing their death and penalty on their behalf.[56] In this way justice has been carried out and all the sins of those who believe have been judged, punished and thus pardoned in Christ Jesus.[57]

In Switzerland, the leading theologian of the twentieth century was Karl Barth (1886–1968). In his atonement theology he emphasized certain aspects, but avoided setting forth a logical atonement theory. He felt that God's acts are so incomparably divine that they cannot be conformed to human reasoning and formulations.[58] His view of penal substitutionary atonement is perhaps best expressed in the following words:

It was we who have deserved death, eternal death. But the Son of God . . . has entered into our place when he became flesh. He has taken to himself the very accusation which was directed against us, the very judgment which was passed upon us. He has borne the punishment which was rightly ours. As the Son of God he

54. Lloyd-Jones, *God the Father, God the Son*, 345.
55. Packer and Dever, *In My Place*, 21–22.
56. Packer and Dever, 22.
57. Packer and Dever, 41.
58. Karl Barth, *The Doctrine of Reconciliation, Part 1*, vol. 4 of *Church Dogmatics*, trans. G. W. Bromiley, eds. G. W. Bromiley and T. F. Torrance (London: T&T Clark, 1956), 80.

could enter into our place, into the place of every individual man, of the whole human.[59]

Barth experienced an uneasy relationship with his contemporary Emil Brunner (1889–1966). Nevertheless, it was Brunner who was quick to point out that "the cross is the only place where the loving, forgiving, merciful God is revealed in such a way that we perceive that his holiness and his love are equally infinite."[60]

The Dutch theologian G. C. Berkouwer (1903–1996) also offered a stunning expression of atonement in his book *The Work of Christ*. He explained that the sacrificial system was imperfect and was never able to effect in any real sense reconciliation between God and human beings because it was only ever a shadow of Christ's sacrifice. Christ presented himself fully in our stead as a substitutionary sacrifice which brought us forgiveness, taking away our sin. This was not a human effort but an act of God, which has effected concrete reconciliation.[61] Berkouwer also noted how Christ's victory is demonstrated in his service, love, meekness and sacrifice. This victory is different because it is the "victorious power of reconciliation and mercy in the way of his suffering and death," even when such a victory was interpreted by the bystanders, as Christ hung on the cross, as a symbol of helplessness.[62]

The Post-Reformation period thus resulted in a bold defence of penal substitution, and yet the Christus Victor theme did also emerge now and again, but seems mostly to have remained in the background.

Next, we will explore the atonement theology of today's prominent theologians. Here we will see a greater emphasis on the Christus Victor theme than we did in the Post-Reformation period.

Today

Many today have become dissatisfied with the theory of penal substitution as a rational and objective view. Yet a polished version of the ancient idea of Christus Victor offers a fresh understanding of the atonement, of Jesus's

---

59. Karl Barth, *The Doctrine of God, Part 1*, vol. 2 of *Church Dogmatics*, trans. G. W. Bromiley, eds. G. W. Bromiley and T. F. Torrance (Edinburgh: T&T Clark, 1957), 152.

60. Emil Brunner, *The Mediator: A Study of the Central Doctrine of the Christian Faith* (Philadelphia: Westminster Press, 1968), 470.

61. G. C. Berkouwer, *Studies in Dogmatics: The Work of Christ* (Grand Rapids: Eerdmans, 1965), 304, 309–10.

62. Berkouwer, *Work of Christ*, 328–35, 338.

full immersion in human experience, in which he shares our struggles, and conquers evil and its power through the resurrection.[63]

Although the Christus Victor theme has to some degree always been present in the church, the idea of Christus Victor in atonement theology today is really about a divine conflict in which Christ the Victor fights and triumphs over the evil powers. It is through Jesus Christ the Victor that God reconciles humanity and the world to himself, which is remarkably different from the idea of satisfaction that we saw earlier. This battle is, therefore, seen as a kind of cosmic battle in which Christ has victory over the evil powers. This victory brings with it a new relationship between God and the world.

Gustaf Aulén (1879–1977), the Swedish theologian who made an important contribution to atonement theology, was right when he said that the Christus Victor theme would experience a fresh emphasis in the years to come, and that it would be seen as a critical part of "genuine, authentic Christian faith."[64]

This is evident in the work of theologians such as Gregory Boyd, who emphasizes cosmic warfare as the framework for the atonement. According to Boyd, Jesus and his first disciples believed that a myriad of spiritual beings populate the universe. Some of these beings are supposedly evil and others are good, and these are at war with one another. Jesus was believed to be the crucial player in this cosmic battle.[65] Boyd observes that a warfare theme runs through Scripture and that the idea of Christus Victor cannot be understood without it. He perceives the biblical narrative to be actually "a story of God's ongoing conflict with, and ultimate victory over, cosmic and human agents who oppose him and who threaten his creation."[66]

Jesus, in bringing the kingdom of God, destroyed death by destroying "the one who has the power of death." This is "the central significance of Jesus's atoning work on the cross and of the resurrection," says Boyd. It was in his atoning work that Jesus established "the kingdom of God and the restoration of a new humanity in the midst of this war zone." Having defeated Satan and having recaptured his rightful rule over all of creation, Christ Jesus is

---

63. Brad Harper, "Christus Victor, Postmodernism, and the Shaping of Atonement Theology," paper presented at the Evangelical Theological Society, 53rd National Conference, Colorado Springs, CO, 14–16 November 2001, accessed 2 July 2011, http://www.tren.com, 5–6, 10.

64. Aulén, *Christus Victor*, 159.

65. Boyd, *God at War*, 238.

66. Gregory Boyd, "The 'Christus Victor' View of the Atonement." Online blog, 2018, accessed 14 October 2022, http://www.gregboyd.org/essays/essays-jesus/the-christus-victor-view-of-the-atonement/.

established as the legitimate King over the cosmos, and humans become his legitimate representatives upon the earth.[67]

According to Boyd, the whole biblical narrative is about "God restoring his creation through humanity," becoming incarnate himself, and defeating his cosmic adversary. Consequently, salvation is an aspect of a universal cosmic restoration, and yet "Christ's cosmic victory results in our personal salvation."[68] Salvation is then most fundamentally about being saved from God's arch-enemy and from the eternal consequences of our sin. Our salvation, then, is to eternally participate in the fullness of life; that is the "joy, power and peace that is the reign of the triune God."[69]

Steve Chalke, also an advocate of the Christus Victor theme, in his book co-authored with Alan Mann, *The Lost Message of Jesus*, illustrates the atonement as follows:

> Just as a lightning-conductor soaks up powerful and destructive bolts of electricity, so Jesus, as he hung on that cross, soaked up all the forces of hate, rejection, pain and alienation all around him. Jesus wasn't failing as the Messiah; he was succeeding. The Kingdom does not come and cannot be maintained by military force. God's Kingdom is established by God's means – self-giving love.[70]

Chalke refers to John 3:16 and finds it difficult to accept that a God who loves the world so much should vent his anger and wrath on his own Son. He says further, "The fact is that the cross isn't a form of *cosmic child abuse* – a vengeful Father, punishing his Son for an offence he has not even committed" (emphasis mine). In strong language he calls such an idea a "twisted version of events [that is] morally dubious and a huge barrier to faith." All the evil powers, both satanic and human, conspired to crush Jesus, but although the cross was a "symbol of failure and defeat," the truth is that it was also "a symbol of love," demonstrating "just how far God as Father and Jesus as his Son are prepared to go to prove that love."[71]

Similarly, Green and Baker feel that penal substitution is a "cultural product" of the West, and according to them it has fallen "on deaf ears in

67. Boyd, *God at War*, 212, 214, 240, 267.
68. Boyd, 113, 250.
69. Boyd, "The 'Christus Victor' View of the Atonement."
70. Chalke and Mann, *Lost Message of Jesus*, 179.
71. Chalke and Mann, 182–83, 191–92.

other social worlds" because of their particular worldview.[72] They believe that the theology of penal substitution has had negative effects in society and has offered little to mission and the church for understanding the message of Jesus, and that the Christus Victor theme has much more to offer.[73] As I hope has been apparent, I hold a very different view, and I will show how both penal substitution and Christus Victor are of vital importance, and are profoundly relevant, for Africans.

John Stott, who was a well-known church leader in the UK, denied that Satan has any rights over humanity which God is required to satisfy. He made it clear that instantly after the fall, Christ's victory was predicted. This victory had its beginnings during Jesus's ministry and "was decisively won at the cross." Stott proclaimed that "the cross was the victory won, and the resurrection was victory endorsed, proclaimed and demonstrated." So, at the very time that Jesus himself was being crushed by Rome, he was actually crushing the serpent's head (Gen 3:15). However, although Satan has been defeated, he has not accepted his defeat and still exercises power. But because Satan knows he is defeated and knows of his approaching doom, his rage is intensified. Although he is defeated, the "painful conflict with him continues." This is why there is tension in both our experience and our theology.[74]

For Stott, the cross is also to be rooted in the holiness of God, who is unable to gaze upon evil because of his infinite perfections. Stott argues that God hates evil and thus his wrath is a holy response to evil, which he could never come to terms with. Because God's eyes are too pure to look upon evil and he is unable to tolerate wrong, our sins separate us from God, and so he hides his face from us. Stott explains that the chief obstacle lies within God himself, and that "he must 'satisfy himself' in the way of salvation he devises; he cannot save us by contradicting himself." Humanity has earned the penalty for breaking the law. God, in condemning it in Christ, justifies us and redeems us because he paid the ransom. Therefore, it was at the cross that "human evil was both punished and overcome, and God's mercy and justice were both satisfied." This satisfaction, though, came from within himself, within God's own nature.[75]

Stott saw the "satisfaction through substitution" as the very centre of Christ's work of atonement, rather than the Christus Victor theme. N. T.

---

72. Green and Baker, *Scandal of the Cross*, 29.

73. Green and Baker, 183, 220–21.

74. John R. W. Stott, *The Cross of Christ* (Nottingham: Inter-Varsity Press, 1989), 265, 274, 279, 289.

75. Stott, *Cross of Christ*, 121, 132, 135, 146, 357.

Wright, one of the most formidable New Testament scholars of our time, takes a different approach. He is inclined to see "the victory of Jesus Christ over all the powers of evil and darkness as the central theme in atonement theology, around which all the other varied meanings of the cross find their particular niche."[76]

Wright therefore proposes that Jesus employed cosmic-warfare language to represent the conflict he himself wrestled with, and that this was ultimately a battle against the evil forces of darkness.[77] The atonement, according to Wright, is not merely an abstract transaction whereby God's forgiveness is given to those who wish to have it; rather, it is primarily a dramatic, explosive achievement in which evil is defeated so that "God's new age could begin."[78] For this reason, Wright argues for "something that can be called 'penal substitution,'" but he regards the Christus Victor theme "as the overarching one within which substitution makes its proper point."[79]

René Girard, a philosopher of social science, offers us a very different approach. He believed that sacrificial scapegoating was a vital part of religion and human society. In view of this, internal conflicts are solved within communities by uniting against a specific victim, be it animal or human. Sacrifice, he believed, is a "primitive artefact of an earlier stage of human development."[80]

Mark Heim, a theologian who developed his theology from Girard, feels that it is a serious mistake to understand sacrifice exclusively in relation to private sin. For him the cross is a sacrifice to end all sacrifices. Effectively, a sacrificial transaction took place at the cross, though it was arranged by human beings, not God. It was God, however, who turned this evil transaction against itself into a saving purpose, whereby the scapegoating system would be overthrown. Heim states that "ransom" is employed to express this idea, and that God pays the ransom price to avoid the shedding of blood of other scapegoats in the future.[81]

---

76. N. T. Wright, *Evil and the Justice of God* (Downers Grove: InterVarsity Press, 2006), 114.

77. Wright, *Justice of God*, 449, 466, 481.

78. Wright, 156.

79. N. T. Wright, "The Cross and the Caricatures: A Response to Robert Jenson, Jeffrey John, and a New Volume Entitled *Pierced for Our Transgressions*," Fulcrum, Eastertide 2007, accessed 18 June 2010, https://www.fulcrum-anglican.org.uk/articles/the-cross-and-the-caricatures/.

80. Mark S. Heim, *Saved from Sacrifice: A Theology of the Cross* (Grand Rapids: Eerdmans, 2006), 15, 23.

81. Heim, *Saved from Sacrifice*, 10, 17, 160–62.

Heim is concerned about the caricature and overly mechanistic features of penal substitution, whereby, according to him, God demands a violent sacrifice or satisfaction. He feels that "it makes Jesus our supreme scapegoat rather than our saviour from sacrifice."[82]

Scot McKnight, however, explains that Jesus knew that he would die, in God's providence, a premature death "at the hands of those who rejected his mission as a potential source of rebellion." Jesus foresaw his death as the consequence of an ordained mission that was all about the inception of the "Final Ordeal," which somehow was connected to God's kingdom.[83]

Having identified with humanity in his incarnation, Jesus incorporates humanity in his victory over the devil and death, and frees those who were held captive by Satan. Furthermore, Jesus became a sacrifice, atoning for the sins of humanity. He died in humanity's stead; our death became his so that his life might become ours. Christ identified with us so that our sins might be removed, and so that he could be victorious "in order to liberate those who are incorporated into him so that they can form the new community where God's will is realized."[84]

It concerns McKnight that a limitation to penal substitution and satisfaction themes would focus exclusively on the "wrath-to-death problem" and the just elimination and resolution of sin. For McKnight, the atonement includes these issues of course, but the atonement is also about recreation. Quoting David Bosch, he says, "Salvation in Christ is salvation in the context of human society en route to a whole and healed world."[85]

Hans Boersma also offers a unique theory of atonement, and yet without a doubt it is characteristic of a harmonization of the penal substitution and Christus Victor themes. He talks about violence and hospitality in God's atoning work, and says that there is a place for both. He says that God came to us in Christ, inviting us into his presence so that we might enjoy eternal fellowship with him. This, Boersma proclaims, "is what atonement theology is all about" – it is "an expression of God's hospitality toward us." Boersma argues that we see divine hospitality in the cross even though divine violence is present as well.[86] It is Boersma's conviction that whatever theme we employ

---

82. Heim, 293–94.

83. Scot McKnight, *Jesus and His Death: Historiography, the Historical Jesus and Atonement Theory* (Waco: Baylor University Press, 2005), 147, 177.

84. Scot McKnight, *A Community Called Atonement* (Nashville: Abingdon, 2007), 107–8.

85. McKnight, *A Community Called Atonement*, 2, 113, 350.

86. Hans Boersma, *Violence, Hospitality and the Cross: Reappropriating the Atonement Tradition* (Grand Rapids: Baker Academic, 2004), 15–17, 51.

in articulating the atonement, God's love must shine through it.[87] Yet he also points out that penal substitution provides significant insight into how one should relate to the social, economic and political realities of everyday life, making choices that involve some degree of violence one way or another.[88]

Boersma believes that the satisfaction or penal substitutionary and moral influence theories are the "means by which God ultimately defeats evil and upholds his eternal and unconditional hospitality."[89] Victory, on the other hand, is the purpose of the atonement. Therefore, one should not divorce these from each other.

Leading on from this idea, Sinclair Ferguson offers the same sentiment. He believes that the multidimensional conflict theme is central in the gospels.[90] Jesus's entire ministry is largely portrayed as a confrontation with Satan. Ferguson points out how Jesus, in Luke 4:1–14, being full of the Spirit, goes into the desert having been led by the Holy Spirit, and undergoes temptation and then attacks it! Therefore, it is not so much that temptation came to Jesus, according to Ferguson. After having entered enemy territory, Jesus comes out from the wilderness as conqueror. This whole episode was "a declaration of war, an attack on the one who claims to be the ruler of this world." In his conquering words "Away from me, Satan" (Matt 4:10 NIV), Jesus demonstrated Satan's defeat.[91]

Throughout Scripture, Ferguson explains, forgiveness of sins through divine justice and Christ's victory over the devil are complementary. Both are fundamental for our salvation and offer a view of atonement from which other aspects may be understood with a deeper sense of richness and clarity. These are profoundly interrelated. According to Ferguson, "any adequate understanding of the atonement must include within it this aspect of Christ's disarming of the power of darkness."[92]

Having explored the atonement in Christian theology, some observations are in order. There is a feeling that the atonement in today's world seeks to offer a solution and hope for the worldwide problem of suffering. The atonement also

---

87. Boersma, *Atonement Tradition*, 112.

88. Boersma, 49, 179.

89. Boersma, 21.

90. Sinclair B. Ferguson, "Christus Victor et Propitiator: The Death of Christ, Substitute and Conqueror," in *For the Fame of God's Name: Essays in Honor of John Piper*, eds. S. Storms and J. Taylor (Wheaton: Crossway, 2010), 171, 176.

91. Ferguson, "Christus Victor et Propitiator," 177.

92. Ferguson, 185.

seems to offer a sense of communal and individual well-being. The atonement theology of today offers a fresh emphasis on Christus Victor, whereby the ancient idea of Christus Victor has been polished and is making its way into a contemporary context. Furthermore, the penal substitutionary theory itself has had to undergo a fresh description, without changing its meaning, as it attempts to engage with the worldview of today.

In this chapter, we have looked at how different theologians in the church have understood the atonement. We have explored atonement theology in the church fathers, the Scholastics, the Reformers and in the Post-Reformation era, and then we have seen how theologians today understand the atonement. While many theologians have had different ideas, the themes of penal substitution and Christus Victor have often been beautifully expressed. One cannot help but appreciate the unique and insightful teachings on the atonement which these theologians have handed down to the church.

However, apart from a handful of church fathers, none of these theologians were African. We might ask, "How does African Christianity understand the atonement today?" This is an important question and I wish to treat it separately, and so we will explore it in the next chapter.

4

Atonement in African Christianity

In the previous chapter, we looked at atonement theology in the history of the Christian church, and how various theologians have understood it. The primary interest of this chapter is to outline the atonement theology of African theologians and church leaders at present. Like the West, Africa also enjoys expressions of atonement which include both penal substitution and Christus Victor themes. Yet there are fewer African Christian theologians and leaders who seek to understand the atonement and publish their work from an African perspective. It is my hope that after reading this book, you will discover situations in an African perspective that are affected profoundly by the atonement.

As in the Old Testament, ritual and sacrifice play a significant role in African culture. It is therefore not surprising that the African theologian Kwame Bediako proclaimed that Christ himself, being sinless and of divine nature, in his incarnation willingly offered himself as a sacrifice to death for humanity's sin and in so doing fulfilled perfectly all that sacrifices and rituals seek to achieve. Furthermore, Jesus is unique, not only because in his divinity he stands apart from us, but also because he has identified with the human predicament by becoming human himself and thus is able to transform it. There is, then, not a single animal or victim that can equal the perfect sacrifice offered by Jesus himself, which is abundantly effective for all peoples everywhere and for all time.[1]

Yusufu Turaki tells us that, as a result of the fall, hostility now exists between God and humanity, and humanity sits under the judgement and

---

1. Kwame Bediako, *Jesus and the Gospel in Africa: History and Experience* (New York: Orbis, 2004), 28–29.

wrath of God; yet these have now been abolished by Christ's work on the cross. Humanity can now enjoy access to God, for Christ has reconciled us to him, and on the horizontal dimension he has reconciled us with one another. Therefore, Turaki sees Christ's atoning work as "the basis of God's willingness to make peace with rebellious humanity and to restore fellowship with man and also to restore his fallen creation." He says that all that was lost or altered at the fall "is now being redeemed and regained through Christ." Touching on the idea of substitutionary atonement, Turaki writes, "Jesus on the cross became our substitute and paid in full the wages of our sins. On account of this, we come to God having nothing to offer him except what Christ effected on our behalf on the cross."[2]

Similarly, when considering African sacrifices, M. Nyeri perceives a difference in the biblical narrative with respect to the concept of atonement. He argues that in Scripture someone else stands on behalf of, or atones for, an offender, and therefore Jesus pays our penalty for sin by standing in our place.[3] Christ's atoning work was more than just a sheer sacrifice! Christ presented an act of atonement for an offence in order to remove guilt. And so, as Turaki points out, Jesus, who is in fact the Righteous Judge, was made sin for us, and in love sacrificed himself by shedding his blood on a cross. While we cannot earn the righteousness of Christ, or his justification, these are mediated to us by means of Christ's substitutionary death. Christ's righteousness is imputed to us through faith and by the ministry of the Holy Spirit.[4]

Turaki teaches that "a Christian and biblical conception of salvation is always universal in scope and application." Turaki does not have "universal salvation" in mind here. But he does say that "the whole world of religions and cultures is invited by Jesus the Messiah to come to him so he can be its Lord and Saviour."[5] African theologians have also considered African philosophy, spirituality and the social influences of their people, and have quite legitimately also incorporated the Christus Victor theme. This theme is rooted in Christ's incarnation. Agrippa Goodman Khathide understands the incarnation as an integral part of God's assault on the powers of darkness, from Jesus's temptation

---

2. Turaki, *Uniqueness of Jesus Christ*, 40–41, 60, 69.

3. M. Nyeri, "A Biblical and Theological Study of the Concept, Meaning and Practice of Atonement in Gong Traditional Religion" (Master's thesis, Jos ECWA Theological Seminary, 2011).

4. Turaki, *Uniqueness of Jesus Christ*, 66.

5. Turaki, 12, 14.

in the wilderness to Satan's defeat at Jesus's death and resurrection.[6] Turaki, in light of African Traditional Religion where humans are responsible for performing the rituals required to restore harmony between themselves and the world of spirits, says that Christians believe that "the Supreme Being took action to restore that equilibrium in the miracle of the Incarnation."[7]

Khathide tells us that "at the cross of Christ, an eternal sacrifice was made, so that humanity's sin might be forgiven and that Satan might be utterly defeated."[8] He continues by explaining how Christ in the gospels is a sacrificial lamb who voluntarily laid down his life unto death, went to hell to atone for the sins of humanity, and rose from the dead as Victor and is now exalted as Lord over the church and the cosmos. Khathide, when considering the apostle Paul's theology, notes that there is "no doubt of Christ's sovereignty and supremacy over the powers," and that Christ defeated the powers of darkness through his death and resurrection. He also acknowledges that the defeat of Satan at the cross did not annihilate or destroy him completely, but rather that Satan has been bound.[9]

In song, African Christians like to sing of the "power in the blood of Jesus" and his victory over infirmities, sickness, blindness, barrenness and evil spirits, and the defeat of Satan. Apparently, when witches come to them, Christians are encouraged to (figuratively) "sprinkle Jesus's blood" in prayer in their homes. Chike explains that Christians in Africa sense that blindness, muteness, barrenness, witches and the devil are all evil forces set against Christians, which they need greater power to overcome.[10] Yet Jesus is more powerful!

The Nigerian novelist Chinua Achebe picked up on this in his classic work *Things Fall Apart*. He wrote of how Africans gave European missionaries a portion of the evil forest, for they knew that the missionaries boasted about victory over death, and they thought this would "give them a real battlefield in which to show their victory." The missionaries, who were unaware of this scheme, were very thankful. The Africans expected that the missionaries would all be dead within four days, and yet none died! "It became known that the

---

6. Agrippa Goodman Khathide, *Hidden Powers: Spirits in the First-Century Jewish World, Luke–Acts and in the African Context*, 2nd ed. (Johannesburg: Acad SA, 2007), 199–202.

7. Yusufu Turaki, *Foundations of African Traditional Religion and Worldview* (Nairobi: WordAlive, 2006), 65.

8. Khathide, *Hidden Powers*, 209.

9. Khathide, 209, 220–22, 224.

10. Chigor Chike, "Proudly African, Proudly Christian: The Roots of Christologies in the African Worldview," *Black Theology: An International Journal* 6, no. 2 (2008): 227.

white man's fetish had unbelievable power. Not long after, he won his first three converts."[11]

Chike observes how many African Christians understand their salvation in terms of victory over evil spirits as well as prosperity and good health. He gives the following examples of definitions of salvation from different African church leaders:

> "Salvation is deliverance from the power of evil principalities and the enclave of human enemies," and salvation is "good health . . . flourishing economic concerns and . . . having children." Or, "where one is in unity with himself, with his neighbours, friends and God, he can say that he is in salvation."[12]

It is no wonder then that many African Christians identify with a Saviour who they believe will provide prosperity, good health, a flourishing economy and deliverance from evil forces.

In African Traditional Religion, salvation is largely understood as achieving well-being and ensuring one's welfare. In such a context, salvation means warding off situations that might diminish well-being and seeking assistance from the spirit world to overcome such impediments so that the fullness of light, mainly in material terms, can be achieved. It is in this context that Africans seek to conquer their fears and to rise to such aspirations. In this philosophical, spiritual atmosphere, "Africa's New Christianity" has been preached with much success, portraying Jesus as fostering material well-being. This promotes the tendency that is already very much alive in the understanding of salvation in the African Traditional Religion, a tendency that has now found its way into African neo-Pentecostal/charismatic Christianity. David Tonghou Ngong explains that Christianity in Africa is about "gaining power to overcome those forces that diminish life" and therefore "material well-being appears to be ultimate in their understanding of salvation."[13]

Nkansah-Obrembong raises a legitimate concern regarding prosperity theology, which he feels is leading the African church "into a philosophy of materialism, which, if not checked, could have devastating effects upon Christianity in Africa."[14] This he thinks may lead to the undermining of the

---

11. Chinua Achebe, *Things Fall Apart*, 50th Anniversary ed. (New York: Anchor, 1994), 149.

12. Chike, "Proudly African, Proudly Christian," 232.

13. David Tonghou Ngong, "Salvation and Materialism in African Theology," *Studies in World Christianity* 15, no. 1 (2009): 3, 10, 14.

14. Nkansah-Obrembong, "Contemporary Theological Situation," 149–50.

Christian teachings of suffering and persecution, which are important to the Christian faith.

African Christians also see Jesus as the "Great Healer." This finds expression in many of their prayers and songs. Faith healing is thus widespread in many African churches. Jesus is also said to be the "Great Provider." How Christian Africans view Jesus is influenced by their understanding of the working of the cosmos and the perception of their needs.[15] Therefore, as Kalu tells us, prosperity theology plays a significant role in African Christianity. This apparently emerges from the notion of salvation and Christ's atoning death, for "African anthropology emphasizes vitality of life and abundant life as the chief goals for daily living. These are the ends of every religious ritual: to preserve, enhance, and protect life."[16]

African Christianity today is undergoing exponential growth especially because of the neo-Pentecostal/charismatic understanding of salvation. This is a serious problem! Ngong shares my concern; he laments that this is because it "treats material well-being as if it were an end in itself." He continues, "African neo-Pentecostal/charismatic Christianity draws from a source that has always informed African Christianity/theology in general: African traditional religious thought." He also feels that an "uncritical appropriation of this salvific discourse [understanding of salvation] undermines the difference within Christianity, thus collapsing Christianity into African Traditional Religions."[17]

On a happier note, Turaki sees that whereas in African Traditional Religion sacrifices and rituals were performed to restore cosmic harmony, Christianity sees God taking action himself to restore this harmony, or equilibrium, through Christ and his incarnation. However, this is not merely a restoration of cosmic harmony – though it certainly is that – but ultimately a new creation.[18]

Africans require a practical solution for their practical problems, which are derived from their unique African perspective. African Christianity has the responsibility to carefully employ that which is of use from African philosophy and spirituality to communicate Christ's atoning work. However, along with other African theologians, we should reject the prosperity gospel and its theology, as it is an unhelpful and inappropriate theology for Africans. In part 2 which follows, I will seek to envision the implications of the atonement in an African perspective. Many of these implications are spiritual and yet also deeply practical.

---

15. Chike, "Proudly African, Proudly Christian," 228–29.

16. Kalu, *African Pentecostalism*, 261.

17. Ngong, "Salvation and Materialism," 1.

18. Turaki, *African Traditional Religion*, 42, 65.

Part 2

5

African Spirituality

Alan Mann talks about creating an atmosphere in which the language of one culture or context is translated into another. He says that in light of Jesus's incarnation, we should take seriously "the need for atonement to be communicated in the context of human culture and language." Mann offers what I believe is a brilliant starting point for part 2 of this book. He writes:

> We need to read and re-read the atonement as time and place changes the context in which we are called to communicate the salvific work of Christ. Our responsibility, as it has been since the paradigmatic intervention of the incarnation, is to discern the overarching predicament of our time, to understand the question behind the questions of our cultural and philosophical context and to engage them with a meaningful and sufficient story of atonement.[1]

The very nature of Christian theology requires that theology developed by African Christians should take the teachings of the wider Christian community into consideration. In so doing, African Christians are able to gain insight into the Christian faith that others have already reflected upon, and thus enrich their own theology. At the same time, there is no doubt that Western Christians could also learn much from their African brothers and sisters. It is, of course, proper to subject one's theology to the Christian tradition throughout history and engage with it in dialogue. Theology, however, becomes more relevant and fruitful if it engages with the recipient culture. Sadly, Nkansah-Obrembong notes that many evangelicals have failed to take African culture seriously, and

---

1. Alan Mann, *Atonement for a "Sinless" Society: Engaging with an Emerging Culture* (Milton Keynes: Paternoster, 2005), 6–7.

that much work is required to work towards a "comprehensive and systematic theology that is biblically and culturally relevant for the church in Africa."[2]

There is an obvious need, therefore, to produce a theology that is uniquely African. But even so, Oden argues that among the fathers of the church, Africa has produced some of the most influential theologians, and their theology plays a "decisive role in the formation of Christian culture."[3] John Mbiti, a Kenyan-born theologian and Christian religious philosopher, believed that Christianity might even be described as indigenous to the African continent. Even before Islam, Christianity was established in Northern Africa, namely in Egypt, Ethiopia and Sudan. Early African Christianity made significant contributions to Christian theology. More specifically, Africa was instrumental in developing the theology of atonement. Nevertheless, it remains the case that in most of Africa today, Christianity is a new religion, and, as Turaki says, this new religion is required to address the same psychological and social concerns of the previous religion, namely, African Traditional Religion.[4] African Christian theology must, therefore, be contextualized, taking into account the African situation. Although this chapter and the chapters that follow are not strictly about African Traditional Religion, I shall draw from its spirituality and cultural beliefs and practices in order to construct an African atonement theology.

In this chapter, I provide an overview of African spirituality intended to offer some important definitions to help us understand the African perspective. It will also provide us with a context in which to place further discussions on the atonement.

The German theologian Jürgen Moltmann correctly understood that "the theology of the cross . . . has cosmological dimensions, because it sees the cosmos in the eschatological history of God."[5] As we shall see, this is remarkably true when we consider the atonement in an African perspective.

Like many other peoples of the world, Africans have reflected thoughtfully on subjects such as God, the nature of personhood, death and immortality, the spirit world, evil, causation, destiny and free will. All of these are important aspects of spirituality for Africans who, by nature, are religious; spirituality fills

---

2. Ibid., 142–144, 149.

3. Thomas C. Oden, *How Africa Shaped the Christian Mind: Rediscovering the African Seedbed of Western Christianity* (Downers Grove: InterVarsity Press, 2007), 9.

4. Turaki, *African Traditional Religion*, 19.

5. Jürgen Moltmann, *The Crucified God: The Cross of Christ as the Foundation and Criticism of Christian Theology* (Minneapolis: Fortress, 1993), 218.

every aspect of their lives. Some of their religious beliefs address the meaning of life, the origins of all things, and death and ultimate existence.

Africans have traditionally understood the universe in spiritual terms. The Western world, however, underwent a philosophical and social revolution which made a forceful distinction between the physical, such as that which can be understood by science, and the spiritual. The Western worldview is foreign to traditional African thought. For Africans, the "physical" and the "spiritual" are tightly interwoven, and this idea of their being interwoven is deeply rooted in their religions and cultural lives.

African Traditional Religion does not have a clear set of written doctrines or strict rules and regulations. Instead, it is an experiential religion that is "more felt than understood." Although African Traditional Religion appears to be in decline as a result of the influences of Christianity and Islam, African spirituality is still very much alive and has significant implications for African Christianity and atonement theology.

The African theologian Yusufu Turaki identifies five aspects that make up the spiritual system of African Traditional Religion: holism, spiritualism, dynamism, communalism and fatalism.[6]

Let's look at *holism* first. In African spirituality holism is closely connected to the cosmos, the beginning and development of creation. According to Turaki, the African worldview considers all things holistically, that is, the sacred and the secular are not distinguished. Turaki says that Africans are more likely to say that "this world in essence is spiritual rather than material and that life is saturated with supernatural possibilities."[7] While there is some truth in Turaki's words, there is causation between the material world and the spiritual in the sense that the two are tightly interwoven into a single fabric. Professor Samuel Kunhiyop thinks that Africans have traditionally rejected the dualist notion which was introduced into many African Christian churches by Western missionaries. This dualist view, Kunhiyop believes, is absent from the Judeo-Christian worldview.[8]

Kwame Bediako calls this a "sacramental universe" in which a sharp dichotomy between the physical and the spiritual is absent. He says, "One set of powers, principles and patterns runs through all things on earth and in the heavens and welds them into a unified cosmic system."[9] My colleague Vernon

6. Turaki, *African Traditional Religion*.
7. Turaki, 33–34.
8. Samuel Waje Kunhiyop, *African Christian Ethics* (Nairobi: HippoBooks, 2008), 66–67.
9. Bediako, *Jesus and the Gospel in Africa*, 88.

Light has developed this idea by saying that there is no division in African Traditional Religion between the sacred and the profane, the invisible and the visible. For Africans, everything is connected to everything else, both above and below, from cosmology to social life, to agriculture, to economics and politics.[10]

Cosmology is profoundly important for Africans, for there exists a close connection between the dependence on nature and an awareness of spirits and spiritual forces, their ancestors and the unity of the physical and the spiritual. No human being is understood as an individual in isolation, but all find themselves in a unified cosmic universe. There is, therefore, a "belief in the divine origin of the universe and the interconnectedness between God, humanity and the cosmos," says Khathide.[11] Africans also view themselves as the centre of the universe, playing a vital part in the "circle of life."

Another significant component of the African spiritual system is *spiritualism*. This includes belief in the African God, sometimes called the Supreme Being, belief in lesser gods, belief in spirits, belief in the ancestors, and practices of medicine and magic. The sense of a very real spiritual dimension is obvious.

Almost all Africans have a pre-Christian concept of God. Some African theologians have argued that this God is the same God as the God of the Bible, and that he fulfils all their religious and cultural aspirations. The characteristics of the African concept of God and the God of the Bible are surprisingly similar. However, there is a vital element that sets the God of the Bible apart from the African God – we will explore this in chapter 7. But for now, in my writing I have chosen to use "God" rather than "god" for both the African concept of God and the Christian God. Sometimes, however, I will use "Supreme Being" interchangeably, to distinguish the African God from the Christian God. From the outset I want to make it clear that I am not suggesting that the two are equal. They are not.

Concerning *dynamism*, Turaki explains that all things in the cosmos, whether nature, humans or spiritual forces, are filled with an impersonal force, a *life force*. Along with this life force, Africans believe that "if humans only knew how to master and control the realm of the supernatural, the world

---

10. Vernon E. Light, "The Evangelical Church in Africa: Towards a model for Christian Discipleship" (extended Master's thesis, Fort Hare University, 2010), 107. See also his *Transforming the Church in Africa: A New Contextually-Relevant Discipleship Model* (Bloomington: AuthorHouse, 2012).

11. Khathide, *Hidden Powers*, 313.

would be a much happier place." Yet this is really a pursuit of mystical and spiritual power, because they hold that their well-being is influenced and controlled by spiritual beings. Therefore, a quest for power would enable them to predict and even manipulate or influence these forces for their own benefit. Usually this is achieved by consulting "specialists who have special means of gaining access to these powers and spirits and may make use of rituals, divination, ceremonies, sacrifices, incantations, symbolism, witchcraft, sorcery, charms, fetishes, and white and black magic."[12] It is this kind of religious atmosphere that helps us understand why the African Initiated Churches and Pentecostalism have flourished on African soil, together with the health, wealth and prosperity gospel.

Communalism, on the other hand, has much to do with the nature of a person and personal identity. For Africans, people do not exist as individuals living independently from one another. Rather, they are interdependent, living together in relationship and community. This is expressed in the African *ubuntu*, which means that "a person is a person through other persons." Yet we must not forget that the African idea of community and relationships also includes the full spectrum of unseen powers and beings, which include the Supreme Being, spirits, ancestors and sometimes even nature.

The last item on Turaki's list of the parts that make up the African spiritual system is *fatalism*. This includes causation, free will and destiny. The idea of fatalism or destiny is tightly connected to spiritualism, for Africans believe that the circumstances in which individuals or groups find themselves are ultimately determined by external spiritual forces. This fatalism is said to be a gift from God, according to Turaki. He tells us that "individuals, families and groups each have their own unique destiny decreed by the Creator and are accompanied throughout life by their destiny spirits." Such destinies can be either known or hidden, and if they are hidden, one can consult traditional diviners, or witch doctors, to discover them. Nevertheless, there are significant theological implications for traditional Africans, for they understandably pursue security and protection to counter the attacks from evil spirits and witches, who seek to change such destinies for the worse.[13]

There is also something called *cosmological balance*. This is the idea of working towards a type of utopia where everything in Africa is in harmony. This is of paramount importance. In the cosmic unity which comprises both

---

12. Turaki, *African Traditional Religion*, 24, 26, 47–48.
13. Turaki, 40–41.

the visible and the invisible, the balance and harmony of all parts is crucial and must be maintained.

If this rhythm of life or cosmological balance is disrupted (and it always is!), negative consequences may manifest themselves, and diviners will be consulted to identify the cause of disharmony. Such causes can include transgression of taboos in a particular society, disrespect, witchcraft and magic.

To restore the balance of such relationships, Khathide tells us that diviners will suggest a remedy appropriate to the cause of the offence. This might be offering a sacrifice or imposing a penalty on the guilty party. The purpose is reconciliation: "to restore harmony or to bring balance or equilibrium back to a person's experience of his or her world . . . is of paramount importance in the African's religio-cultural reality."[14] We shall explore this further in chapter 14, *Cosmic Harmony and an African Hope.* But in the next chapter we will look at the fascinating topic of atonement in African Traditional ritual.

---

14. Khathide, *Hidden Powers*, 316.

6

Atonement in African Traditional Ritual

In the previous chapter we examined African spirituality, which has laid the foundation for the discussions which follow. In this chapter I want to be somewhat specific and talk about atonement in traditional African rituals. We will see that African spirituality significantly influences the traditional understanding of atonement in sacrifice and ritual.

Community is fundamental to the African understanding of being. If an individual commits a sin or an offence, the whole community suffers guilt, because that individual does not live in isolation but is bound by the rules, regulations and taboos of the community.

Professor James Nkansah-Obrembong explains that even though Africans may not understand sin in theological terms, they see it as a falling short of social ideals, and therefore sin is not only a personal offence but one that affects society. Shame brought about by sin might be felt by the individual, but usually is experienced by the whole community as well. Considering the implications of sin, Nkansah-Obrembong continues,

> Sin disrupts the social order and therefore carries social implications for the individual or the community. Sin is an evil that upsets society's equilibrium as well as personal relationships and the cosmic relations such as the spirit world, the ancestors and nature. Thus sin's effects extend even to the cosmic realm.[1]

---

1. James Nkansah-Obrembong, "Sin in African Perspective," in *Global Dictionary of Theology: A Resource for the Worldwide Church*, eds. W. A. Dyrness and V. Kärkkäinen (Downers Grove: InterVarsity Press, 2008), 825–26.

Whether communities, families or individuals commit sin, fines and penalties must be paid to compensate for their offences. Such a penalty or fine is meant to be equal to the offence committed, and it removes the guilt of the offence when the penalty is paid. This is often done through ritual. It is usually the duty of the chief, the elders of the clan or a traditional priest to determine the penalty for an offence. This might be an animal sacrifice, a meal, drink offerings or offerings of certain objects. With respect to an animal sacrifice, a priest kills the animal, takes its blood and sprinkles it on certain objects of ritual or on the ground as a means of appeasing the ancestors, the spirits or God. The penalty then releases the offender from the curse of his or her offence. In many instances of African sacrificial ritual, an animal suffers and dies on behalf of the offender, similar to what we saw in the sacrifices of the Old Testament.

My wife, Catherine, used to live up in the mountains in the eastern equatorial regions of South Sudan. While working there for six years as a missionary among the Lopit tribe she witnessed exactly this approach to offences, in a way that was specific to the tribe among which she worked. She told me about one instance where a young man seduced and had sexual intercourse with a young unmarried women. In this tribe such an offence was taken very seriously. After the man was caught, the elders of the village enforced a penalty on him to atone for his offence. His family had to pay for a bull on his behalf and offer it to the girl's father as compensation. In a separate incident, a man betrayed his tribe. This was an offence against the whole community, and therefore the penalty was much more severe. He had to pay twenty cows for every family! Fortunately for him, he had a wealthy uncle who was able to pay for the cows on his behalf. In this case, however, the recompense did not stop there. After the cows were paid for, the elders of the village and the betrayer sat in a circle to take part in a ritual of reconciliation. As they sat in solemn silence, they passed a calabash bowl filled with water to every member of the circle and each in turn took a deep sip and then spat back into the mix. After this ceremony, the traditional priest, or some similar figure, sprinkled the mixture around on the ground of the central meeting place where tribal dances took place. At this point the ritual was complete and the offender was reconciled to his community. Actually, the story did not end there; some years later there was a severe flare-up. This was before Catherine and I were married, when we were in frequent communication via Skype. Without going into all the details, just before the tribunal, Catherine and I met on Skype and were able to find a solution to bring reconciliation through the atoning work of Christ at the tribunal where several villages were present. The outcome and reconciliation in Christ were simply spectacular! There is no doubt that there are many other instances in African traditional sacrifice and ritual where penalties are paid by a type of substitutionary atonement.

Klaus Nürnberger explains that for traditional Africans, life is largely ritualized "because reality consists of dynamistic power flows that need to be monitored and kept in check or channelled in desirable directions."[2] Atonement is therefore usually made to avoid misfortune and evil during the here and now, should an act of sin or offence have been committed. Africans petition God to save them from evil in order that they might have peace and abundant life.

For the traditional African, sacrifice is a means of ensuring a peaceful relationship between a living community and the wider community of nature, ancestors, spirits and God, the Supreme Being. The problem is not so much whether the sacrifice is sufficient – though that is an issue too – but whether it accomplishes its purpose. J. Omosade Awolalu makes this clear when he points out that behind a sacrificial offering "there is usually a definite purpose. There is no aimlessness in making an offering, and we assert that no one ever makes a sacrifice without having a goal in view."[3] The goal is almost always to counteract evil or unwelcome forces. However, various theories to explain the purpose of sacrifice have been suggested, namely, the thank offering, the gift offering, communication and propitiation.[4] Although I believe many of these overlap, I think the propitiation theory is most significant.

The first of the sacrificial theories is the thank offering, which is used to hold communion with the Supreme Being or other deities and the ancestors. Like many African rites, the sacrifices of thanksgiving are often accompanied by feasting, where the people and the spirits who receive the offering share a common meal. The gift offerings are often offered up to maintain cosmic harmony. According to the communication theory, traditional Africans also offer sacrifices to communicate with the spiritual and mystical forces. The purpose is usually personal, and might include protection, security, success or favour from the spirits or the ancestors.

The propitiation theory, as I said, is particularly important. For many Africans a penalty paid in terms of a substitutionary sacrifice for an offence may appease the offended spirit, warding off misfortune due to them as the

2. Klaus Nürnberger, *The Living Dead and the Living God: Christ and the Ancestors in a Changing Africa* (Pietermaritzburg: Cluster Publications, 2007), 38.

3. J. Omosade Awolalu, *Yoruba Beliefs and Sacrificial Rites* (New York: Athelia Henrietta Press, 1996), 138.

4. Tokunboh Adeyemo, "The Doctrine of God in African Traditional Religion" (PhD diss., Dallas Theological Seminary, 1978), 173, available at www.tren.com; Awolalu, *Yoruba Beliefs*, 143.

consequence of an offence. Writing about substitutionary sacrifices among traditional Africans, Tokunboh Adeyemo explains,

> Under this category sacrifices are offered when a person is believed to be under the wrath of the divinities or some malignant spirits. The end of his trouble would be death; but such a sacrifice, if offered according to prescription, would save him. What is offered therefore is a substitute for him. Almost in every case, a sheep is the victim used as substitute for a human. The sheep is rubbed against the body of the suppliant to ensure the transfer of his destiny, as far as the illness and imminent death are concerned, to the sheep. Then the sheep is treated like a corpse and buried with funeral rites as if it were the suppliant.[5]

There are incredible parallels between Adeyemo's explanation and the Old Testament Day of Atonement and Jesus being "the Lamb of God, who takes away the sin of the world" (John 1:29). A substitutionary sacrifice is employed to propitiate the anger of the spirits, ancestors or divinities. This is especially appropriate when Africans experience an outbreak of plague, a famine, crop failures, sudden deaths or other disasters, all of which are attributed either to the anger of those who dwell in the spirit world, or to an error or violation in a religious ritual committed by a human being. Usually, the cause of the disaster is sought in order to make good by a propitiatory sacrifice, which is said not only to purify individuals and the community, but more importantly to turn the favour of the offended ancestor, spirit or deity back towards the people.

It is no surprise that blood plays an important symbolic role in traditional African religions. Turaki says that "ritual sacrifices and the use of blood are believed to empower those who perform them. The sacrificed meat or food is eaten in a prescribed manner, and so is the blood."[6] Nyeri records the use of a blood ritual in an African community after the offence of adultery had been committed. He explains that the "blood of the he-goat would be taken to the house of the priest or an elder and be sprinkled on the *walls and the door posts*. The same is also taken to the house of the male adulterer and sprinkled all over his house" (emphasis mine).[7] The imagery here reminds us of the blood of the Passover lamb in Exodus 12:1–28.

---

5. Tokunboh Adeyemo, "African Traditional Concept of Salvation in the Light of Biblical Teaching" (Master's thesis, Talbot School of Theology, 1976), 32, available at http://www.tren.com.

6. Turaki, *Uniqueness of Jesus Christ*, 92.

7. Nyeri, "Gong Traditional Religion."

Another Old Testament atonement theme reflected in African traditional ritual is the scapegoat (see Lev 16:21–22; 23:27–29). Awolalu explains that it was once a practice among some Africans to employ a human scapegoat who would carry away diseases, sins and even death in the community. "This human scapegoat was known as *Tele*. The Edi purificatory rite lasts seven days." On the last day, the *Tele* would be carried away as a "special burden" and would be ritually tied. Through this ritual it was believed that calamities, misfortunes and sins were transferred onto the human scapegoat who was ceremonially carried away into the grove where he would be offered up.[8] The sacrificial scapegoating played a significant part in some African communities and sought to deal with the internal conflicts within such communities by uniting against a scapegoat.

Further, traditional sacrifices and rituals are employed to secure future prosperity. The practice of making sacrifices and offerings is common to most, if not all, traditional Africans and has the main concern of pursuing harmony. However, the concept of cosmic harmony has an even greater ultimate end, the goal of prosperity and well-being. Adeyemo believes that "sacrifices are offered to meet personal needs, such as security, protection, communication, success, and favour of the gods."[9] Bénézet Bujo also points out that the repetition of traditional rites and formulae expresses the faith of the African people that their ancestors will bring them prosperity and ward off misfortune. These rituals, he says, are a means of remembering and re-enacting the past and securing prosperity for later generations.[10]

For Africans, such traditional sacrifices and rituals die hard. Christ dying for the world over two thousand years ago appears to have little meaning for many Africans, at least in terms of the Christian doctrines of the West. Africans require a practical solution to their practical problems. Ritual and sacrifice fulfil these needs. I believe that African Christians should use those things which are useful and biblical from within their African spirituality and culture to communicate the gospel without practising syncretism or compromising the gospel truth. African Christianity therefore has the responsibility to employ wisely that which is of use from African spirituality to communicate Christ's atoning work.

---

8. Awolalu, *Yoruba Beliefs*, 179–80.

9. Adeyemo, "Doctrine of God," 176.

10. Bénézet Bujo, *African Theology in Its Social Context*, trans. J. O'Donohue (Eugene: Wipf & Stock, 1992), 29–30.

7

The Problem of the African Idea of God

African cosmology is the system by which Africans incorporate the mystery they experience in their "unseen" lives, acknowledging the "beyondness" of human life. It also refers to how Africans relate to the cosmic forces, that is, how they perceive their lives in relation to unseen beings. These unseen beings might include God, sometimes referred to as the Supreme Being, and intermediaries like ancestors and other spirits. Within this cosmic arrangement, Africans feel that they are not left to face life and its troubles alone. They appeal to God for help, but more often than not they relate to him through intermediaries like ancestors and other spirits. In this chapter I explore the African concept of God. Often I will refer to the African idea of God as the "Supreme Being." We will begin by looking at the nature of the African God, and then we will explore how we should approach such a God in light of Jesus Christ and his atoning work. This is important because it provides a background from which to envision the cross of Christ in an African perspective.

The idea of an African pre-Christian concept of God is no longer disputed, for God has long been a vital part of African spirituality. Even well before the arrival of Christian missionaries in Africa, most tribes acknowledged a Supreme Being, as expressed in religious ceremonies, myths, proverbs, short sayings, prayers and even song. While it is still possible that one might find some African people groups who have no awareness of a Supreme Being, almost all Africans take God for granted; there is no need to prove to them that God exists. For Africans, God is prominent and permeates every aspect of thought and daily life.

For the many Africans who have a strong belief in God, they say that he is everywhere at all times. He is greater than everything that he has created,

75

which is why he is called the Supreme Being, and yet at the same time God is near to his people, so close that they are able to approach him. While some people might disagree with this, we will see shortly why and how God is in fact approachable.

While Africans believe in God, they also believe in other spiritual beings, some of which are closely associated with the Supreme Being. Some African theologians, such as John Mbiti, Bénézet Bujo and Bolasi Idowu, have thought that the African concept of God is not dissimilar from the Judeo-Christian God, at least as revealed in the Old Testament. The proclamation of the Christian gospel, according to Bujo, was not a new presentation of the concept of God, but instead a "more complete and definite proclamation of that one God, whom Africa already knew."[1] Other African theologians argue otherwise. Yusufu Turaki says that the traditional African idea of God "is not narrowly defined. God may be viewed in a pantheistic, polytheistic, anthropomorphic manner, as a Supreme Power or a Supreme Being."[2]

Nevertheless, we can affirm that the Supreme Being and the Judeo-Christian God are similar in some ways. Both are supreme in their universe, and both are the source of life, "the foundation and explanation of all creation and existence," as Kunhiyop puts it.[3] Africans have special names for God. These names, Agrippa Khathide says, illustrate a "continuity of God between the pre-Christian era and the period of Christian missionaries,"[4] because most of these names have been employed by both traditional Africans and Christians. Furthermore, J. Omosade Awolalu describes the Supreme Being as "all-wise, all-knowing, all-seeing and all-hearing."[5] In the same way, Kunhiyop describes the attributes of the Supreme Being as "being the creator, King and judge who is omnipresent, omnipotent, all-wise, all-knowing, all-seeing and immortal." He is morally good, merciful, loving and holy, and upholds governance and justice. It is he who provides children, good harvests and protection. As God himself is good, he expects his created beings to be good towards one another as well.[6]

Traditional Africans generally understand that God is both transcendent and immanent. However, God's transcendence, that is, his remoteness, should not be interpreted as isolation, as in Western theology, but rather "in terms

---

1. Bujo, *African Theology*, 18.
2. Turaki, *African Traditional Religion*, 57.
3. Kunhiyop, *African Christian Ethics*, 16.
4. Khathide, *Hidden Powers*, 317–18.
5. Awolalu, *Yoruba Beliefs*, 15.
6. Kunhiyop, *African Christian Ethics*, 16–17.

of a holistic cosmic community in which there is some kind of hierarchy of beings," says Turaki.[7] The Supreme Being, while said to be very far away in one respect, is at the same time very near to his creation. As judge, guardian and sustainer, God is said to be sovereign over all and above all. But Sawyerr points out that God also takes an active interest in the affairs of people, acting as their vindicator, "the relative who is prepared to expose himself to any risk in order to protect a weaker member of his family." Yet as Creator "he is also believed to be remotely situated from the everyday events of human life."[8] Mbiti thinks that any notion of the African concept of God as being too remote or excluded from human affairs is entirely false,[9] because God, in the African mind, is simultaneously transcendent and immanent, far and near. Prayers, sacrifices, offerings, and so on, are notable acknowledgements of God's immanence, and so in theory God is transcendent, but in practice he is immanent, according to Mbiti.[10]

Considering the idea of God as an ancestor, Nürnberger writes, "The Supreme Being can also sometimes even be seen as the ultimate Ancestor from whom all ancestry is derived."[11] With God as an ancestor, people can turn to him in times of anguish, but as we have seen, he is also transcendent, separate and distinct. Sawyerr says that God is the father of the ancestors: he is their Great Ancestor, the Ultimate Ancestor, because he is the source of all being and of all existence and value.[12] It is in light of this that I believe that God can be (or is) understood as both Creator and Ancestor by almost all African people. Yet we will see in the next chapter that I take a similar, though somewhat different, stance, and this will be important for understanding the cross of Christ in an African perspective.

Despite some differences, similarities do exist between the African understanding of God and the Old Testament concept of God. As I have already suggested, these similarities might include God's omnipresence, omnipotence, omniscience, immortality, benevolence, mercy, loving-kindness, provision, protection, life-giving power, governance, justice, and God as Creator, the source and origin of all things. Although Turaki accepts these similarities, he

---

7. Turaki, *African Traditional Religion*, 55.

8. Harry Sawyerr, *God: Ancestor or Creator? Aspects of Traditional Belief in Ghana, Nigeria and Sierra Leone* (London: Longman, 1970), 5.

9. John S. Mbiti, *African Religions and Philosophy*, 2nd ed. (Oxford: Heinemann Educational, 1989), 32.

10. John S. Mbiti, *Concepts of God in Africa* (New York: Praeger, 1970), 12, 17–18.

11. Nürnberger, *Christ and the Ancestors*, 34.

12. Sawyerr, *God: Ancestor or Creator?*, 31.

thinks that the traditional African view of God and the biblical Christian God are in reality grounded "in radically different theological foundations."[13] Yet both Mbiti and Idowu, in order to defend their people against the accusation of not having a concept of God, pioneered the idea that the African God is, in fact, the same God as the God of the Bible, only pre-Christian. Turaki charges them with falling into the Western philosophical and theological trap of employing its terms to interpret and articulate the traditional ideas of the African God. Byang Kato, a pioneer of contemporary African evangelical scholarship, praised Mbiti's ground-breaking work *Concepts of God in Africa* as "highly commendable." Yet he perceived that Mbiti's presuppositions inevitably affected his interpretation of his data, especially where there was a lack of clarity in certain African beliefs. Mbiti, Kato says, sought to highlight the African view of God as a "preparation for the gospel," convincing his readers that Africans had always known and worshipped God, even if it was a pre-Christian God.[14] This therefore begs the question: Is the African concept of God the Christian God? The answer, I believe, is no. But the traditional African understanding of God does point Africans to the God of the Bible.

As Adeyemo observes, "while the natural revelation may enable Africans to attain knowledge of God as the Creator of all things, it does not provide them with the knowledge of such mysteries as the Trinity, the incarnation, and redemption."[15] Kunhiyop, in his *African Christian Theology*, writes that the practices and beliefs of African Traditional Religion at best offer only a pale and incomplete understanding of who God is. He continues, "The only true source of knowledge about the Christian God is his personal revelation of himself in Jesus Christ and the recording of that revelation in the inspired, inerrant and infallible Holy Scriptures."[16] Similarly, the Western theologian D. A. Carson explains that it is Scripture that tells us about God and the kind of God he is, and while a dim representation of his "moral attributes [is] reflected in the human conscience," this knowledge is insufficient to lead anyone to salvation.[17] If we wish to understand the cross of Christ in an African perspective, we cannot rely on the traditional views of an African God, for Christ is absent from such a God. Martin Luther claimed that a true knowledge of God comes

---

13. Turaki, *African Traditional Religion*, 53.

14. Byang Kato, "A Critique of Incipient Universalism in Tropical Africa" (PhD diss., Dallas Theological Seminary, 1974), 108–9.

15. Adeyemo, "Doctrine of God," 62.

16. Kunhiyop, *African Christian Theology*, 44.

17. D. A. Carson, *Collected Writings on Scripture*, compiled by Andrew David Naselli (Wheaton: Crossway, 2010), 19–20.

only through Jesus Christ, and that apart from Christ any encounter with God would be disastrous. Luther once said, "God himself is a terrible God if we want to deal with him apart from Christ. He is a God in whom we find no comfort, but only wrath and displeasure."[18] Carson writes, "This Son-centred revelation is found not only in the person of Jesus but also in his deeds. Not only in his teaching, preaching, and healing, but supremely in the cross and resurrection Jesus reveals God and accomplishes the divine plan of redemption."[19]

The atonement is the factor that distinguishes the God of the Bible from the African idea of God. Therefore, we need to understand the atonement, the cross of Christ, not in light of the African view of God, but in light of the God of Scripture. Although the traditional African God is in some ways similar to the Christian God, he is ultimately a very different kind of God. He is a God without Christ! Therefore, the atonement is the distinguishing factor between the God of the Bible, who atones for the sins of his people and overcomes evil, and the African concept of God, the Supreme Being who is a non-atoning God.

I mentioned above that I would address the whole aspect of God being the Ultimate Ancestor, and so in the next chapter I will discuss how Jesus Christ relates to the ancestors.

---

18. Luther, quoted in Allison, *Historical Theology*, 199.
19. Carson, *Collected Writings*, 21.

8

Christ and the Ancestors

To begin, I must introduce the idea and function of intermediaries, or mediators, of whom ancestors are a part. In African life the function of intermediaries is crucial. The duty of an intermediary is to form a "bridge" between human beings and the Supreme Being.

There are two classes of intermediaries. The first class consists of those who are still alive physically, those whom you can touch. Such mediators might include kings, chiefs, elders, diviners, seers, witch doctors, medicine men, oracles, ritual elders and rainmakers. The second class of mediators is those of the spirit kind. These include divinities, or lesser gods, spirits and ancestors. All kinds of intermediaries are relevant for traditional Africans. I will not deal with every African intermediary. However, I hope that after reading this book you will know how to deal with each of them in light of Christ's atonement. Here I focus attention on the ancestors, because they are most central to African culture and traditional religions.

Because Africans understand the Supreme Being to be supremely transcendent, they feel the need to approach him via an intermediary. A person might approach a chief through someone of higher status than him- or herself. I like to use the example of a child in a village who has been unfairly mistreated by an older person. The child wishes to take the matter to the chief of the village, who has the authority to bring justice, but although the chief is near, living just a stone's throw away, his social status makes him unreachable for the child. So the child approaches his father and begs him to approach the chief as an intermediary on his behalf. Africans approach God in a similar way, by means of intermediaries.

Adeyemo explains that in the traditional arrangement, power and authority are "exercised through the chiefs and priests believed to be divine representatives on earth. In the spiritual world, the divinities and ancestors channel the power."[1] Therefore, people go to mediators to offer up prayers, offerings and sacrifices after telling them their needs.

Ancestors are sometimes called the "living dead" and are believed to still be very much a part of the community of the living. Ancestors are also said to be the spirits of the elders of a village who have died. They are, according to Reed and Mtukwa, "guardians of morality in the community." If members of a community "diminish the life force of the community" by committing an offence, the ancestors may afflict them with tragedy or disaster. Yet blessing follows those members of a community who please the ancestors. A contradiction of fear and fondness towards their ancestors often exists among many Africans.[2] Clark explains that the relationship the ancestors have with the living community demonstrates that ancestorhood is an extension of one's living parents. Ancestors engage with their communities in parental fashion. Punishment is administered to those who disobey and disrespect them, and health, prosperity and protection are offered to those who honour them. There is, therefore, a reciprocal obligation on the living and the "living dead."[3] However, Agbonkhianmeghe Orobator explains that Africans care little for the ancestors of other communities, because they are not *their* ancestors, and foreign ancestors have no influence in a community. A community celebrates its own ancestors and does not recognize a foreign ancestor. Foreign ancestors are "merely unfamiliar spirits floating above human existence."[4]

The ancestors are considered to be benevolent towards their own people when the people fulfil their obligations. Accordingly, Khathide remarks that ancestors have never been thought of as evil spirits.[5] Nonetheless, Light writes that there is literally a price to be paid for a friendly intervention by the ancestors. The ancestors must frequently be thanked by means of offerings and sacrifices; the people should pray to, honour, respect and obey them, in order to experience benevolent intervention from the ancestors.[6]

---

1. Adeyemo, "Doctrine of God," 116.

2. Rodney Reed and Gift Mtukwa, "Christ Our Ancestor: African Christology and the Danger of Contextualization," *Wesleyan Theological Journal* 45, no. 1 (2010): 150.

3. Jawanza Eric Clark, "Reconceiving the Doctrine of Jesus as Savior in Terms of the African Understanding of an Ancestor: A Model for the Black Church," *Black Theology: An International Journal* 8, no. 2 (2010): 152.

4. Agbonkhianmeghe E. Orobator, *Theology Brewed in an African Pot* (New York: Orbis, 2008), 114.

5. Khathide, *Hidden Powers*, 337.

6. Light, "Evangelical Church in Africa," 105; see also his *Transforming the Church in Africa*.

The great African theologian Kwame Bediako also points out that "ancestors are considered worthy of honour for having 'lived among us' and for having brought benefits to us."[7] It is believed, therefore, that ancestors should be honoured and respected, and for good reason. They occupy a privileged position due to having distinguished themselves in service and having lived exemplary lives within their communities before their passing. It is this privileged position that enables the ancestors to act as mediators and intercessors on behalf of their living community members. The ancestors are therefore entitled to libations, prayers, offerings and sacrifices.[8] Another characteristic of ancestorhood is simply their close proximity to the community. As ancestors are still in essence people, they are thought to be the best-suited intermediaries between God and human beings. Having recently been human beings themselves, they know the needs of their people. While ancestors are close to the communities from which they came, and are thought to still live among them, they also enjoy close proximity to the Supreme Being. Africans are under severe "pressure to ensure their dead relatives achieve and maintain ancestorhood, as well as to do everything possible to attain and sustain ancestral status themselves after their death," says Light.[9] On this point Bujo tells us that "communion with the ancestors has both an eschatological and a salvation dimension." This salvation concerns both the living and the "living dead," for their actions affect one another in a "salvation" sense and thus they are mutually dependent.[10]

As ancestors are both part of their communities and nearer to God, they have the ability to, as it were, be "bilingual." They communicate in the language of human beings, of whom they were a part, and also in the language of the spirits, of which they are now a part. While the living communicate with their ancestors by means of ritual offerings, sacrifices and invocation, the "bilingual" communication of the ancestors often manifests itself in the dreams or visions of the living.

Furthermore, Bediako explains that traditional Africans believe that the welfare of society depends on preserving good relations with their ancestors, on whom they depend for protection and assistance. Good relations may be preserved by the use of traditional rituals which ensure "the maintenance of the desired harmony between the living and the ancestors."[11] Turaki writes,

7. Bediako, *Jesus and the Gospel in Africa*, 30.
8. Orobator, *Theology Brewed*, 75.
9. Light, "Evangelical Church in Africa," 107; see also his *Transforming the Church in Africa*.
10. Bujo, *African Theology*, 24.
11. Bediako, *Jesus and the Gospel in Africa*, 101.

> When misfortune strikes, those affected should examine their
> conduct toward their kinsfolk and neighbours to see whether they
> have failed to fulfil any duties and obligations. Any act of sin or
> moral wrong should be *atoned for*, often through the sacrifice
> of an animal or fowl. Some offences also require the *payment
> of fines*. Forgiveness takes effect immediately after restitution or
> *reconciliation*. In this way quarrels between individuals, families
> or communities are settled through *reconciliation*. *Peace-making*
> and treaties are conducted under oaths and vows which are usually
> *sealed by blood sacrifice* [emphasis mine].[12]

My emphasis in Turaki's quote highlights several themes covered in part 1 of
this book. This causes us to consider the parallels with Christ's atoning work.
We will return to this shortly.

With respect to the blurring of ancestral worship and veneration that is
sometimes felt, one might wish to remove ancestors from African culture.
Kwabena Asamoah-Gyadu regrets that evangelical Protestant Christianity "has
often rejected any considerations for the recognition of ancestors in African
Christianity."[13] This is especially true among adherents of Pentecostalism: belief
in the power of ancestors is assumed by many to be demonic and pagan. It is felt
that they should have no place within the lives of born-again Christians. African
theologians hold different views when it comes to engaging with ancestors.
For example, Bediako argues that studies on African Traditional Religion
have illustrated that these religions are not "passive traditional cosmologies,"
but being "dynamic institutions" they are "able to adapt and respond to new
situations and human needs in society."[14] Bujo thinks otherwise. He says that the
ancestors are central to both African spirituality and African social structure,
and that to remove the ancestors from African thought would damage the
entire fabric of society.[15] It also concerns Orobator that Africans have men
and women who have gone before them, whose lives were exemplary and who
still watch over them and love them, and who are now closer to the Supreme

---

12. Turaki, *African Traditional Religion*, 69.

13. J. Kwabena Asamoah-Gyadu, "'The Evil You Have Done Can Ruin the Whole Clan':
African Cosmology, Community, and Christianity in Achebe's *Things Fall Apart*," *Studies in
World Christianity* 16, no. 1 (2010): 53.

14. Kwame Bediako, *Christianity in Africa: The Renewal of a Non-Western Religion*
(Edinburgh: Edinburgh University Press, 1995), 212.

15. Bujo, *African Theology*, 41.

Being.[16] I believe that we should take both positions into consideration. In a moment I shall propose a third option, one that I hope will position Christ at the very centre of African life and spirituality.

Some Roman Catholics have attempted to integrate ancestral belief into the doctrine of the Communion of Saints in order to address the ancestral issues at hand. As African ancestors fulfil certain qualifications in order to receive the status of mediator, so too do the canonized Catholic saints, who are officially proclaimed mediators or intercessors. Like Catholics, who honour and celebrate their saints, so too Africans celebrate and honour their people who have lived exemplary lives, argues Orobator, a Jesuit priest from Nigeria. He continues, "The lives of these saints and ancestors challenged us to become living saints, that is, men and women whose lives are an example for others to imitate."[17] Joseph Healey and Donald Sybertz, who are also Roman Catholic priests who have worked in Africa for many years, describe the saints in Catholicism as special "Christian ancestors." This, they believe, "is an illumination and enrichment of traditional African beliefs and a new and higher synthesis for African Christianity and the world church."[18] Roman Catholic churches in Africa have, therefore, not surprisingly "incorporated the veneration of the African ancestors in their liturgy."[19]

I am in agreement with Bujo. I fear that the belief in ancestors is so deeply rooted in African culture and spirituality that it would buckle the whole social structure of countless African communities should it be removed. If such a shift in African culture and belief were to occur, it would need to come from Africans themselves. While I am not Roman Catholic, and neither do I wish to embrace the integration of ancestral belief into the doctrine of the Communion of Saints as presented by Orobator and Healey and Sybertz, I do commend the Roman Catholic Church for their ingenuity and sensitivity. They seem to have done much more than Protestants to engage with ancestral belief.

In light of the above, I contend that African communal ancestors should not be done away with. Africans should acknowledge their ancestors, in a similar way, perhaps, to how we might honour and respect the authors and heroes of Scripture, significant figures in church history and other heroes of the Christian faith. Africa has enjoyed some of the finest theologians and church

16. Orobator, *Theology Brewed*, 117.

17. Orobator, 118.

18. Joseph Healey and Donald Sybertz, *Towards an African Narrative Theology* (New York: Orbis, 2004), 28.

19. Healey and Sybertz, *African Narrative Theology*, 216.

leaders in Christian history – for example, Origen, Athanasius, Clement, Augustine, Tertullian, Cyprian – as well as the great African church leaders and theologians of today. Many of them feature in this book. These were, and are, exemplary Christians whom the African people can honour and celebrate as well.

It fascinates me that Jesus himself exhibits almost all the positive attributes of the African ancestor, but displays them in such an extraordinary, spectacular way that it seems to diminish the need or even the desire to approach any other intermediary for mediation and intercession. Thankfully, I seem to be in good company. No sooner had I articulated my own thinking here, than I discovered Kwame Bediako's reassuring words: "Once Jesus Christ comes, the ancestors are cut off as means of blessing and we lay our power-lines differently."[20]

The structure of the world of spirits and its mediators, as Africans understand it, forms the setting in which to display the extraordinary attributes of Christ and his atoning work. It is, therefore, my hope that Africans will bypass their ancestors and other intermediaries as a means of mediation, while still honouring and celebrating the lives of those who have gone before them. Perhaps such celebrations could be expressed through dance, song and feasts. Nevertheless, this should be done without syncretism or ancestral veneration.

Nyende explains that the author of Hebrews presents Christ as a mediator, even as a high priest, which itself is a concept of Jesus Christ from within Jewish religious thought. This seems to suggest a biblical legitimacy for a conceptualization and interpretation of Jesus which can be easily grasped.[21] Perhaps for Africans, Jesus could be conceptualized as an African ancestor.

Many Africans understand God as a Supreme Being, and sometimes even as the Great Ancestor. It would therefore be appropriate, I believe, to think of Jesus as the Supreme Ancestor, because Jesus in his incarnation is fully human and yet also fully God. The African philosopher Kwasi Wiredu writes, "If an ancestor is a ruler, the scope of his activities goes beyond his own family to the whole of his town or kingdom."[22] If we are to think of Jesus as an ancestor, in fact the Supreme Ancestor, then Wiredu's words are profound, because Jesus's rulership is universal; it is without end (John 18:36–37; Heb 1:1–4; 2:5–12)! Jesus can thus be the Supreme Ancestor of all peoples, not just the peoples of

20. Bediako, *Christianity in Africa*, 217.

21. Peter Nyende, "Why Bother with Hebrews? An African Perspective," *The Heythrop Journal* 46, no. 4 (2005): 519.

22. Kwasi Wiredu, "Death and the Afterlife in African Culture," in *Person and Community: Ghanaian Philosophical Studies 1*, eds. K. Gyekye and K. Wiredu (Washington: Council for Research in Values and Philosophy, 1992), 137.

Africa, because the whole world, the whole universe, belongs to Christ; it is his kingdom. Yet, although Jesus can be thought of as an ancestor, by contrasting Jesus, the Supreme Ancestor, with ordinary ancestors we shall see that he is a very different kind of ancestor. In fact, ordinary ancestors can themselves receive salvation only through the Supreme Ancestor and his atoning work.

Turaki takes a different point of view. He believes that "Jesus cannot take a seat in the gallery of religious mediators; He is not one of them. He is different and unique. He does not have their likeness and cannot be likened to them."[23] While it is correct to say that Jesus is different and unique, for indeed he is God, Turaki forgets about Jesus's incarnation when he says, "He does not have their [the ancestors'] likeness and cannot be likened to them." It is precisely because of Jesus's incarnation (John 1:14; 18:37; Gal 4:4; Phil 2:7) that we can, and should, in an African perspective, speak of Jesus as the Supreme Ancestor. He took on humanity and dwelled among us: therefore Jesus in this sense is most certainly like any African person! Again Turaki tells us, "Jesus the Messiah is neither an ancestor nor 'one of them.' He did not originate from within human nature. He is its creator."[24] I agree that Jesus is the Creator of all, including the ancestors. Jesus, being divine and eternal, did not originate from creation, and yet he was born of a virgin (Matt 1:18–25), which in itself is grounds to consider Jesus not only as an ancestor, but as the Supreme Ancestor! Turaki is, however, on firmer ground when he writes,

> We do not make Jesus the Messiah look like one of the ancestors, but he can be presented symbolically as one who fulfils the aspirations of those who depend upon the ancestors and therefore stands as their Mediator. Our knowledge of the status, role and functions of the ancestors can help us grasp even more the deep theological and the biblical meaning of Christ's mediatory role in African societies.[25]

To avoid venturing into the territory on my own, it would be good to consider the position of other African theologians on Christ being an ancestor. Reed and Mtukwa mention that Bediako thinks of Christ helping Africans understand their "natural" ancestors. Bediako wrote, "An Ancestor-Christology in African theology is meant to show that Christ, by virtue of his incarnation, death, resurrection and ascension into the realm of spirit-power, can rightly

---

23. Turaki, *Uniqueness of Jesus Christ*, 22.
24. Turaki, 24.
25. Turaki, 24.

be designated, in African terms, as Ancestor, indeed Supreme Ancestor."[26] An Ancestor-Christology, according to Bediako, helps make clear the position and significance of "natural" ancestors. "By making room among the 'living-dead' for the Lord, the judge of both the living and the dead, it becomes more evident how they relate to him, and he to them."[27]

Furthermore, Reed and Mtukwa note how Bujo "cautions that the term ancestor should be used analogically since to treat Jesus otherwise would be to make him only one founding ancestor among many." For Bujo, "ancestors are forerunners or images of the Proto-Ancestor, Jesus Christ." He emphasizes that Jesus as the Proto-Ancestor sets the benchmark for what a good ancestor is.[28]

Reed and Mtukwa are somewhat critical, however, of Bediako's "Ancestor-Christology" and Bujo's "Proto-Ancestor." They "find that the image of Christ as Ancestor has an inherent weakness with regard to ethnocentrism." Africa is in desperate need, not of a Jesus shaped in an African image, but of an Africa shaped in Jesus's image.[29]

What I would like to do is first demonstrate how Jesus as Supreme Ancestor does not contribute to ethnocentrism, but actually quite the opposite. And second, I will propose that Africa can be shaped in Jesus's image only once it is able to identify him within its own worldview. Indeed, Jesus makes himself accessible by identifying himself with us by becoming man in his incarnation. The world and spirituality in which Africans live and think make Jesus as Supreme Ancestor a suitable means by which he makes himself accessible to Africans by identifying himself within their worldview.

Reed and Mtukwa offer additional concerns that are understandably shared by many others as well. We need to deal with these fairly. The first concern is that Christ as an ancestor might encourage Africans to continue to treat their ancestors as intermediaries, when it is taught in Scripture that there is only one mediator, Jesus Christ (1 Tim 2:5). Second, it might encourage ancestral offerings and sacrifices that lead to ancestral worship. A third concern is that it might make Jesus a mere human being instead of God incarnate. Lastly, Scripture condemns necromancy.[30]

---

26. Bediako, quoted in Reed and Mtukwa, "Christ Our Ancestor," 153.
27. Bediako, *Christianity in Africa*, 217.
28. Reed and Mtukwa, "Christ Our Ancestor," 154; Bujo, *African Theology*, 76, 79; Orobator, *Theology Brewed*, 76.
29. Reed and Mtukwa, 162.
30. Reed and Mtukwa, 157.

I think it would generally be agreed that these concerns are legitimate, but let us think a little deeper. First, a proper understanding of Jesus Christ and the atonement would diminish the need for any other mediator and would set him apart as sole mediator. With respect to the second concern, if it is properly understood that Christ is infinitely superior to any ancestor and that ancestors acquire their salvation through Christ if they have believed in him as Lord and Saviour, then I do not see ancestral worship being an issue. Third, we should understand Jesus as fully human anyway, yet it is as important to understand him as divine, fully God. The last concern is that necromancy is condemned by Scripture, which is true. However, as I will show, if Christ is truly the Supreme Ancestor, there is no need to communicate with the dead – or even for the dead to communicate with the living! Necromancy becomes obsolete.

Nevertheless, let us consider for a moment some remarkable similarities that Jesus shares with the ancestors. First, like the ancestors, Jesus is worthy of honour (John 5:22–23; Heb 3:3–4), for he not only lived among us, but also brought benefits to us. Turaki explains that Jesus "was found worthy by God and was thus made the Mediator and Reconciler between God and man," and that the apostle Paul also found Jesus to be worthy because of his humility and atoning work.[31] Second, like the African ancestors, Jesus tells us that he is always with us and that he will never leave us. So he too lives among us in our communities (Matt 18:20; 28:20; John 14:18–20; Heb 13:5). Third, Jesus cares for all these communities and has their best interests at heart (Matt 5:13–16; Mark 3:7–14; John 13:34–35). Fourth, Jesus is kind, indeed infinitely kinder than any African ancestor who is said to be kind (Matt 9:36; 10:8; 11:5; 14:14; 20:34; John 15:12–14). Fifth, just as the living and the "living dead" experience communion and fellowship together according to traditional African religion, so too we are called to enjoy communion and fellowship with Jesus Christ (1 Cor 1:9; 1 John 1:1–2). Lastly, Jesus is a mediator, as are ancestors, according to traditional Africans. I shall develop this point shortly.

Despite such similarities, however, the superiority of Jesus Christ as the Supreme Ancestor over and above African ancestors is profound! African ancestors are said to be mediators, and while Jesus is also said to be a mediator, he makes every other intermediary weak and redundant on account of his infinite power and superiority. Unlike African ancestors, Jesus "is the superior Mediator by virtue of his Deity and work of redemption. The religious practices, rituals, worship and sacrifices of all religions and cultures fall under this super

---

31. Turaki, *Uniqueness of Jesus Christ*, 36.

work of Christ" (1 Tim 2:5; 1 John 2:1–2; Heb 8:6–7; 9:9–14; 12:24).[32] As Nyende points out, "Jesus' superior mediation is on the basis of who he is, and what he has done,"[33] and Hebrews 2:5–18 clarifies this. Accordingly, in the African context Christ becomes the ultimate mediator.

The origin of African ancestors is purely human. The Supreme Ancestor, on the other hand, is divine; he is God (Matt 28:19; Mark 1:1–3; John 1:1–18; 5:17–18; Phil 2:5–6; Col 1:15–16; Heb 1:6, 8)! This puts Jesus as an Ancestor in a very different position from any other ancestor.

Although there is confusion about whether ancestors are worshipped or venerated, it is generally understood that they should be venerated rather than worshipped, and indeed ancestors, while they require veneration, do not require worship. There is no question, on the other hand, that Jesus the Supreme Ancestor should be worshipped by all people and all spirits (Matt 2:2, 11; 14:33; 28:9, 17; Luke 24:52; John 9:38; Heb 1:6). In fact, as we read in Revelation 5:11–14, all the "spirits," or angelic beings, worship Jesus on account of his atoning work, which by his blood and sacrifice ransomed people for God.

Although ancestors lived admirable, moral lives worthy of honour, being human they were by no means sinless. In fact, Scripture makes it quite clear that no human being except Jesus Christ is without sin (Rom 3:23; 3:10; 1 John 1:10). The Supreme Ancestor, Jesus, is wonderfully unique, for he is entirely sinless; he has never known sin (1 Pet 2:22; Heb 4:15). Jesus's sinlessness makes him infinitely more powerful than, and superior to, any other ancestor or intermediary. The worth of a sacrifice offered by a sinless being is, of course, boundless! Second Corinthians 5:21 explains that it was because of the sin of humanity that Christ, who knew no sin, took all the sin of the world upon himself and was made to be sin so that in him we might become the righteousness of God. In this way, Jesus the Supreme Ancestor presents himself as the penal substitutionary offering for us. Not only is Jesus without sin, but he also came so that he might take away our sin and offences (1 John 3:5). All other ancestors are unable to take away people's sin because they themselves are inherently sinful. Despite their "admirable," "moral" lives, their sin means that they have practised lawlessness (1 John 1:10; 3:4).

Like the Supreme Being, Jesus, the Supreme Ancestor, who is God himself, is all-powerful. We read in Psalm 110 and Hebrews 2:14–15 of Jesus's power: that through his death he utterly destroyed the devil and that one day he will

---

32. Turaki, 108.

33. Peter Nyende, "Hebrews' Christology and Its Contemporary Apprehension in Africa." *Neotestamentica* 41, no. 2 (2007), 367.

destroy every rule, authority and power until he has placed all his enemies under his feet. The last enemy that God will destroy is death (1 Cor 15:24b–26).

The apostle Paul tells us in Ephesians 1:18–23 of Christ's immeasurable greatness and of his power towards those who believe, but he also provides us with a Christocentric interpretation of Psalm 110. Here he gives an expansive description of the spiritual forces subjected to Christ, and of how Christ is seated at God's right hand, having a status that is above all rule, power, authority and dominion. No ancestor or African claims such prominence, omnipotence and rulership!

Furthermore, African ancestors were born as human, meaning, of course, that they have a beginning. The Supreme Ancestor, however, is eternal on both sides of the continuum – past and future. He is always existent, without beginning and without end (John 1:1–2; 8:56–58; 17:5; Heb 1:2; 13:8; Rev 1:8; 22:13).

We saw above how Reed and Mtukwa expressed concern regarding ethnocentrism when thinking of Jesus as an ancestor. However, as we read in John 10:16 and 12:32, Christ unites all peoples, both Jews and Gentiles, by drawing all people to himself. Second Corinthians 5:18–19 also shows us that through the atoning work of Jesus Christ the Supreme Ancestor, all the world has been reconciled to God. This is beautifully reiterated in Revelation 5:9, where we may understand that Jesus is the Supreme Ancestor common to "every tribe and language and people and nation." Here Jesus is unusual because he is not a local ancestor. By no means! He is the supreme, universal Ancestor for all communities. Remember Wiredu's words we quoted above: "If an ancestor is a ruler, the scope of his activities goes beyond his own family to the whole of his town or kingdom."[34] The rulership of Christ is not local. No, it is supreme and universal. It is cosmic!

Although African ancestors, according to African Traditional Religion, offer salvation in terms of protection, security and aid, this salvation is almost always uncertain and unfruitful: even in the eyes of Africans. Christ the Supreme Ancestor, on the other hand, provides an eternal salvation that is both certain and effectual (John 3:16; 5:24; 10:13, 28; Heb 9:12–15; 1 Pet 3:18–22; 1 John 5:11–13). Further, ancestors require frequent offerings and sacrifices to evoke their kind intervention. Christ, on the other hand, did the unthinkable and offered *himself* as the offering and sacrifice for us (Eph 5:2). And, having been made like us in our humanity in every way, he made himself a propitiation for our offences (Heb 2:17). Therefore, by the sacrifice of his own

---

34. Wiredu, "Death and the Afterlife," 137.

blood, not by goats and calves, Jesus secures an eternal redemption, becoming a new intermediary, and a very different kind of mediator (Heb 9:12–15; 1 Pet 1:18–20) from African intermediaries. Now, because of Jesus's superiority and power, there can be only one mediator (1 Tim 2:5). Consequently, Jesus presents himself as the Supreme Ancestor who becomes the offering and sacrifice, and because he takes it upon himself to offer a sacrifice of unequal worth, he makes the work of all other ancestors, intermediaries, offerings and sacrifices redundant, for he is infinitely greater (Heb 10:12–14).

The Christus Victor theme is explicit in Jesus's resurrection. His infinite power and superiority as the Supreme Ancestor is sealed and justified through his bodily resurrection. Not a single ancestor has ever undergone bodily resurrection after death. In fact, ancestors are said to exist in spirit form among their communities. Conversely, Jesus was resurrected bodily (1 Cor 15; 1 Pet 3:21–23). This too places Jesus Christ in the status of Supreme Ancestor, for he alone has literally conquered death (Luke 24:46–47; John 11:25–26; Rom 6:4, 9; 1 Cor 15:3–5; Phil 3:10; 1 Pet 1:3). Further, his resurrection as the "firstfruits" is a promise that through his offering and sacrifice, his atoning work on the cross, he will one day likewise resurrect our bodies, offering us imperishable salvation (1 Cor 15:35–58)!

In this chapter I have sought to avoid a compromise or even a synthesis between African Traditional Religion and orthodox Christianity. Rather, I have placed Jesus Christ in the very centre of the African worldview and spirituality, and watched it come to life as Christ himself restructures it for his glory. I have also showed how the superiority of Jesus Christ through his atonement makes the intermediary work of all other mediators redundant, and presented Jesus Christ as the Supreme Ancestor, the ultimate sacrifice and the ultimate saviour. The implications of this offer a conception of Christ that is easily accessible to Africans and presents them with the hope of redemption. In the next chapter we will consider how the cross of Christ overcomes evil spirits in Africa.

9

The Cross of Christ and Evil Spirits

I grew up in Umtata, Transkei. The Transkei is a rural part of South Africa which was once a homeland before it became part of the Eastern Cape. The traditional religion and culture of the Transkei were, and in many ways still are, very strong. I remember as a child often hearing all sorts of strange stories about African spirits, almost all of which were evil. Perhaps the most infamous was the Tokokloshe, which is feared in many parts of South Africa. The Tokokloshe is a hairy dwarf-like humanoid which wanders about during the night and is quite a frightful little being. He is believed to be a mischievous evil spirit which creates havoc in the home and is said to cause harm, sickness and even death: he also takes pleasure in frightening little children.

At the age of about eight, I remember going to visit the home of our domestic worker with my mother. The first thing I noticed as I walked in was a brick under each leg of the bed, raising her bed an extra few inches. This, they say, protects a person while sleeping. I suppose the Tokokloshe, being as short as he is, cannot reach a bed that is ten centimetres taller than himself.

The Tokokloshe is one of countless evil spirits in Africa, and while I might not believe in the Tokokloshe or the African perception of evil spirits that many Africans find so terrifying, I do believe that Satan and demons exist, so let us not be too quick to discredit the African fear of evil spirits. In this chapter I want us to consider evil spirits as they are understood by Africans, and to see them in light of demons, or the evil spirits that we read about in Scripture.

Like intermediaries, spirits and spirit possession are a part of many African traditional cultures and spiritualities. There is apparently a great variety of spirit beings, and many of them are evil. Some of these evil forces are harnessed by witches and wizards to accomplish wicked deeds. Yet, on the other hand, according to many Africans, people can enter into a relationship with good spirits and share in their blessings and power, receiving their protection from evil forces.[1] I must state here that forming a relationship with any spirit other than the Holy Spirit, good or evil, is sinful and should never be done by any sincere Christian. Ultimately, it is believed that evil spirits are a major factor in social disharmony, causing fear, sickness, poverty, barrenness and misfortune.

In African belief, evil spirits, although often powerful, are by no means omnipotent like the Supreme Being. They are in fact inferior to him. They are, however, said to be powerful enough to provoke people to commit evil deeds, and are capable of inflicting fever and insanity. Bujo explains that individuals are always anxious about protecting their lives, and their families, against the attacks of evil spirits. Apparently such evil spirits can be appeased by making special offerings through a traditional specialist, often a witch doctor. Africa has produced complex systems of rituals to protect life from such evil. As a result, there is an intense preoccupation with such things which haunts the lives of countless Africans. The terror of evil spirits is not unique to African life, but is evident throughout the Bible as well (1 Sam 16:14; Matt 4:23–25; Mark 1:21–26; Luke 9:37–43; 4:33–41; Acts 5:16; 8:6–8; Rev 18:2).

The concept of Satan in Africa is also interesting. Khathide has argued that in Africa there is hardly an equivalent for the biblical concept of Satan, resulting in Bible translators in Africa leaving "Satan" untranslated; they simply Africanize "Satan." Khathide, having surveyed some of what could be referred to as African representations of the Christian concept of Satan, finds no figure in Africa that is comparable to the devil as found in the Christian Scriptures.[2] I, however, think that Africans do have a very real sense of a satanic figure that is much like Satan, or the devil. Mbiti likewise explains that some Africans personify evil itself. For an example he looks to the Vugusu, who talk of "an evil divinity which God created good, but later on turned against him and began to do evil (see Ezek 28:12–19; Isa 14:12–15; Luke 10:18). This divinity is assisted by evil spirits, and all evil now comes from that lot."[3] While this might have come from early missionary influences, Adeyemo makes a similar observation of the Yoruba, who are a major ethnic group in West Africa. He writes that the Yoruba identify one of their divinities as "the Devil" (Esu) and that this divinity is described much like Satan in the biblical narrative.[4] Furthermore, Parrinder, remembering the words of "William Bosman, a Dutch traveller to the Guinea Coast in the early eighteenth century," writes, "The Devil is annually

---

1. Kunhiyop, *African Christian Ethics*, 18; Bediako, *Jesus and the Gospel in Africa*, 87.
2. Khathide, *Hidden Powers*, 356–57.
3. Mbiti, *African Religions and Philosophy*, 199.
4. Adeyemo, "Doctrine of God," 38.

banished from all their towns with an abundance of ceremony, at an appointed time set apart for that end."[5]

Further, spirit possession in the African context shares similarities with the biblical accounts. However, in Africa, according to Khathide, spirit possession is not always to be feared, but is sometimes desirable, and is often induced by ritual activity, drumming and special dancing. However, negative possession is said to result in insanity and illness. Khathide highlights the negative effects of possession when it is viewed as undesirable and harmful (not that I think there are any instances of possession that are unharmful!), "driving the possessed person to leave home so that they live in forests, when it causes them to jump into the fire and get themselves burnt or torture their bodies with sharp instruments or harm other people" (compare Matt 17:14–21; Mark 5:2–5; 9:15–29; Acts 19:13–16). The spirit that forces such behaviour is considered antisocial.[6] Nevertheless, Jesus understood himself to be in a battle against the evil forces of darkness, and ultimately has victory over them. A typical, parallel example is of when Jesus arrived in the country of the Gerasenes and a man possessed by evil spirits, who dwelled among the tombs on the mountains, came to meet him. The Gospel of Mark records that the demoniac used to cry out and cut himself with stones, and that no one could subdue him (Mark 5:1–20). But in Mark 5:9–13 Jesus assumes his role as Christ the Victor and overpowers the evil spirits who called themselves "Legion" (for they were many), and casts them out of the man and into a herd of pigs. When African people are possessed like the Gerasene man, exorcism is sought from traditional witch doctors and diviners. Usually such exorcism is carried out during formal ceremonies to drive out the malevolent spirits. Turaki significantly notes that while evil spirits may possess people and inflict disease and suffering, they can be appeased through sacrifices and offerings.[7] Aside from exorcism, Africans also seek to protect themselves from such spirits by wearing protective paraphernalia, such as charms and amulets.

The early missionaries to the African continent came with the intention of proclaiming the gospel, but unconsciously "demonstrated ignorance in understanding and dealing with spirits and spirit possession," says Khathide.[8] Today, however, the African Initiated Churches and African Pentecostal/charismatic churches do engage with the issues of possession and exorcism.

---

5. Geoffrey Parrinder, *African Traditional Religion* (Westport: Greenwood Press, 1976), 14.

6. Khathide, *Hidden Powers*, 364, 368.

7. Turaki, *African Traditional Religion*, 65.

8. Khathide, *Hidden Powers*, 358.

Khathide observes that "prayers for deliverance from demons and harmful spirits are offered at many church services even during the week." He also comments that there has been phenomenal growth in African churches of faith-healers and ministers who offer deliverance from evil spirits.[9] Some time ago, as I was walking in the streets of Nairobi, I came across two so-called "Christian" pamphlets being sold by a street vendor. Out of interest I purchased both of them: one was titled *How to Identify and Break Curses* and the other *How to Discover and Deliver Devil Worshipers.* Aside from the fact that the author wanted the reader's money at the end of the pamphlet and assured the reader that *he* had the power to deliver and break curses, his theology and use of Scripture were highly questionable, to say the least! Of course, I have been arguing in this book that the cross of Christ alone is what frees us from all curses; it is Christ who delivers us, not any human being.

Kalu sees in African Pentecostalism a renewal of the African social system which seeks to critique and redefine "possession." An alternative is provided: a "white," clean possession by the Holy Spirit is now popular. Therefore, Pentecostalism (and, I might add, African Initiated Churches and charismatic theology in Africa) offers a new form of possession which replaces the old spirit possession so common throughout Africa.[10]

For many African churches, demonic possession and exorcism are still a significant part of African Christianity. As a case in point, exorcisms are featured almost always in the rituals and liturgy of the Redeemed Christian Church of God (RCCG). Some elements of traditional African cultural practices are thought to be severely demonized, and are viewed as responsible for poverty, sickness, barrenness, misfortune and countless other difficulties. Opportunity for deliverance and protection from evil spirits can be found within the RCCG by way of exorcism, says Ukah.[11] Another example is a church called Mountain of Fire and Miracles (MFM), currently one of the largest Pentecostal churches in Nigeria, which apparently offers "a deliverance ministry *par excellence.*"[12] Titles of MFM publications include the following: *Dealing with the Evil Powers of Your Father's House, Overcoming Witchcraft, Dealing with Local Satanic Technology* and *Power against Marine Spirits.* Such

9. Khathide, 374.

10. Kalu, *African Pentecostalism*, 172.

11. Asonzeh Franklin-Kennedy Ukah, "The Redeemed Christian Church of God (RCCG), Nigeria. Local Identities and Global Processes in African Pentecostalism" (PhD diss., Kulturwissenschaftliche Fakultät der Universität Bayreuth, 2003), 269.

12. Richard Burgess, "Freedom from the Past and Faith for the Future: Nigerian Pentecostal Theology in Global Perspective," *PentecoStudies* 7, no. 2 (2008): 37.

publications provide a detailed liturgy of prayers to free Christians from evil spirits and remove barriers to personal prosperity and development. This is a reflection of MFM's "preoccupation with deliverance from witchcraft and evil spirits, as well as past associations with 'occult' powers and traditional religious culture."[13] Doubtless, this emphasis is not peculiar to the RCCG and MFM ministries, but is evident in countless Christian churches and ministries throughout Africa, especially where RCCG, MFM and others have significant influence throughout the continent. Unfortunately, however, because the "spiritual warfare" emphasis is largely founded on the charismata without the necessary theological training, many "ministers" promote the demonization of almost everything and everyone. This often results in hurt and the embarrassment of those who seek their help.[14]

In African Traditional Religion, as noted earlier, evil spirits can be appeased by making offerings and sacrifices through a traditional specialist, healer or witch doctor. These rituals provide not only exorcism, but also protection from evil spirits and their harassment. For it is believed that the people concerned have committed offences or sins against the spirits. But we must remember Jesus's penal substitutionary death, whereby sins and offences have been paid for in full by Jesus's sacrificial death on the cross! Certainly, the payment was not made to any evil spirit, but such a payment made by God himself on our behalf settles the matter. Evil spirits are inferior to God anyway, and therefore do not have a claim on any Christian. Romans 8:1 makes this clear: "There is therefore now no condemnation for those who are in Christ Jesus."

The good news is that there is no need for sacrifices and offerings to appease any spirit. Those who have put their faith in Christ and his gospel are set free from evil spirits. We can begin to see how Jesus's death was a victory over sin and evil spirits. Here we see how penal substitution and the Christus Victor theme work together! The African theologian Kwame Bediako expressed it well:

> The church must manifest the victory of the cross in the concrete realities of her existence in society, and demonstrate that she has begun to be liberated from bondage to the "powers" that rule existence and the cosmic order in that context. Christian conversion and Christian conviction need to find concrete expression in relation to the "elemental forces."[15]

---

13. Burgess, "Nigerian Pentecostal Theology," 37.
14. Khathide, *Hidden Powers*, 374.
15. Bediako, *Jesus and the Gospel in Africa*, 106.

By now we can appreciate that Africans view life as a spiritual battle. It is for this reason that Africans look to a warrior to assist them. Therefore, African Christians look to Jesus as the Victor who overcomes the powers of darkness and offers freedom from fear, as we saw in the biblical account regarding the Gerasene demoniac. According to Healey and Sybertz, Jesus is the "Liberator" and the "Conqueror of evil powers." They tell us that "in the African cultural context, Jesus overcomes the malevolent powers of the evil spirits and witches. Being concerned with the whole person, he frees the fearful, heals the sick, feeds the hungry, and helps the poor."[16] Likewise, Bediako assures African Christians that in their life struggles Jesus goes ahead of them and "he alone is capable of fighting and conquering, leading his people in triumph." He believes that the "incarnation and the victory of the cross" are together made meaningful in defeating the terrors of the African world, in both the physical and the spiritual worlds.[17] Not only this, but Christ, through his victorious death and resurrection, also overcomes the terror experienced by many Africans, and in his victory he offers them freedom from fear.

Bediako says that, first, above everything else, Jesus is seen by African Christians as Christus Victor, for he is supreme over all spiritual rule and authority. This perception, Bediako says, originates from the intense "awareness of forces and powers at work in the world that threaten the interests of life and harmony." Since Jesus is victorious over evil spirits, he meets the African need for a powerful protector. Second, the idea of Jesus as Saviour for the African Christian "brings near and makes universal the almightiness of God."[18] Christ is able to do all things, and is able to save in all situations to protect against evil spirits. Let us not undermine the power of Christ and his spectacular atonement when it comes to the victory over evil spirits.

Such an understanding of the cross of Christ provides a remarkable theology for African Christians who struggle with fear and affliction on account of evil spiritual beings. Not only has Jesus offered a supreme sacrifice for all the sins and offences of the Christian, but also he has overcome the power of all evil spirits. Christ alone is able to cast out evil spirits, and his victory over them is once and for all (Matt 8:16–17, 28–34; 12:22; Mark 1:21–26, 29–33; Luke 6:17–19; 11:14; Acts 10:38). African Christians can now live in freedom from fear, because sin, death and Satan no longer have a hold on them, for Christ has been victorious and has paid the penalty!

---

16. Healey and Sybertz, *African Narrative Theology*, 300.

17. Bediako, *Jesus and the Gospel in Africa*, 9–19.

18. Bediako, 22.

10

The Cross of Christ and Sin

In the previous chapter we looked at the cross of Christ and evil spirits. In this chapter we will consider another aspect of evil, sin, and how the cross of Christ overcomes it. As you might have figured, sin in an African perspective is usually understood somewhat differently from the understanding of sin in a Christian worldview.

The consequences of original sin in Genesis 3 are clearly revealed in many African struggles. Universal sin has its origin in the garden of Eden, sometimes called "the fall." The origin of "African sin" is no different. Adeyemo has written that "myths and oral traditions abound in African stories about the fall of man and the separation of heaven and earth."[1] However, an African understanding of sin in light of African culture and spirituality may differ somewhat from a strictly biblical concept of sin. Despite this, I hope to demonstrate that it is not as different as one might suppose.

In African spirituality, sin is viewed as largely cosmological, that is, it is caused by external forces which include "principalities and powers." The forces are said to be in disharmony with nature. Nevertheless, African spirituality also acknowledges human sin. For traditional Africans, communal sin is emphasized above personal sin. As J. Omosade Awolalu explains, "Africans do not have a rigid distinction between an offence committed against a person or society and one committed against a God or other divinities and spirits."[2]

Nonetheless, throughout the African continent there are various myths and legends that indicate that there once existed a "Golden Age" when all things were in a state of harmony and bliss. These myths, according to Kunhiyop,

---

1. Adeyemo, "Concept of Salvation," 19.
2. J. Omosade Awolalu, "Sin and Its Removal in African Traditional Religion," *Journal of the American Academy of Religion* 44, no. 2 (1976): 279.

"give glimpses of the separation of God from human beings."[3] There previously existed a close connection between heaven and earth, whereby "man could go to God in heaven and return to earth as he wished, and when he did not need to work before he had his daily bread supplied by the Supreme Being."[4] However, disobedience entered this world and something went seriously wrong! In his *Concepts of God in Africa* the African theologian Mbiti offered numerous examples from different African societies of stories about the fall and original sin. Many of these myths speak of "the coming of death to men to his anger [sic], provoked by the disobedience of the first men." The Supreme Being, who once dwelled upon a paradise earth among human beings, "in a great rage of fury" punished the inhabitants of earth with death for their disobedience and then withdrew himself from them. As a result, humanity now experiences sorrow, misfortune, calamities and death.[5] In some African oral traditions there is an even stronger parallel to the biblical account:

> In one Bambuti myth, it is narrated that when the first men ate the fruit which God had forbidden them, he became so angry that he sent death among them. . . . The Chagga have similar stories, in which they tell how the first men made God angry through eating the forbidden yam, and twice again through their wickedness.[6]

Arno Meiring explains that what traditional Christianity abstractly calls "sin" or "evil" is better expressed in African Traditional Religion by the concept of "wrongdoing," "badness" or "destruction of life." In Africa, sin depends on a particular community's norms and context, rather than an otherworldly standard. The African perception of morality is largely tangible and pragmatic.[7] Mbiti expounds on the African consciousness of sin by explaining that morals are usually written on their minds and consciences by their upbringing and their observations of what members of their community do and do not do.[8] Light also points out that sin is not against the Supreme Being, but against the community and its ancestors; it is a breach of "the unity and harmony between members in the community or between humans and the spirit

3. Kunhiyop, *African Christian Theology*, 69.

4. Awolalu, "Sin and Its Removal," 282.

5. Mbiti, *Concepts of God*, 37, 117.

6. Mbiti, 97.

7. Arno Meiring, "As Below, So Above: A Perspective on African Theology," *HTS Teologiese Studies/Theological Studies* 63, no. 2 (2007): 740.

8. John S. Mbiti, *Introduction to African Religion*, 2nd rev. ed. (Oxford: Heinemann Educational, 1991), 178.

world."[9] Nürnberger also says that "African" sin is not committed against God, nor is it even a transgression of a moral code: instead, it is believed to be a "breakdown of the complex structure of human relationships within the community including the ancestors." The effects of such evil, Nürnberger explains, may be dealt with only by means of "elaborate rituals in which the offender, the offended, the living community and the deceased are reconciled with each other."[10] Adeyemo wrote, "Sin is chiefly an offence against one's neighbour and it is punishable here and now."[11]

However, Bolasi E. Idowu says, "One element of God's justice that is emphasized very much, of which Africans are ever-conscious, is that of 'the Wrath of God.'"[12] This, he explains, is conceptualized by cultic objects in some African shrines. Contrary to Light, Adeyemo and others, this presupposes that sin or "wrong deeds" are ultimately committed against God, even though punishment may be meted out by divinities or the ancestors.[13] So there seems to be agreement with the African myths of "the fall" after all! In the end, the biblical and African concepts of sin are not too dissimilar, even though they might look a little different on the surface.

The concern for African communal harmony is rooted in Africans' perception of community being the theatre for the activity of humans as well as the integrity of African communities, which is more important than that which is abstract and does not originate from within the community.[14] Turaki states that in African Traditional Religion an action is said to be sinful if it fails to promote cosmic harmony.[15] As Meiring puts it, "sin creates imbalance in the relationship between God and man or between man and man. Such imbalance is usually attended by catastrophe not only to the offender but also to the whole community."[16] Adeyemo explains that sin upsets the "equilibrium of society" and personal relationships. Yet for Africans the consequences of sinful behaviour extend into the world of spirits; the cosmic order is disturbed by acts of sin.[17] As a result, Awolalu says, sin "drives a wedge between man" and

---

9. Light, "Evangelical Church in Africa," 131. See also his *Transforming the Church in Africa.*

10. Nürnberger, *Christ and the Ancestors*, 28.

11. Adeyemo, "Concept of Salvation," 71.

12. Bolasi E. Idowu, *Olódùmarè: God in Yoruba Belief* (London: Longmans, 1962), 164.

13. Awolalu, "Sin and Its Removal," 287.

14. Meiring, "As Below, So Above," 739.

15. Turaki, *Uniqueness of Jesus Christ*, 46.

16. Meiring, 739.

17. Adeyemo, "Concept of Salvation," 47.

the spiritual world. For this reason traditional Africans do all they can to satisfy God and his intermediaries, and to live in obedience to the standards of their particular society. Sin is a grave concern for Africans, and so "they attempt to remove the stain and blemish which sin impresses upon them as individuals or as a community."[18] To put it simply, salvation is cultural acceptance by the living community and the ancestral community. It is a social salvation.

Some truth can, however, be found in the African myths. The offence committed by humanity leading to God distancing himself parallels the biblical account. Africans do not seem to offer any suggestion as to whether God (or humankind) has made, or will make, an attempt to restore this separation from God and restore harmony. Nor do these myths offer any explanation for how evil originated in the human heart. As Mbiti observed, the African myths do not point us to a solution for how death might be overcome or removed from the world, and how the earth might once again enjoy a sinless state of paradise and bliss.[19] Yet the cross of Christ offers a profound solution.

Professor Kunhiyop explains that "wrongdoing will always bring negative consequences until atonement is made." In African Traditional Religion, therefore, sacrifices are made in an attempt to reconcile the wrongdoer with the recipient(s) of the offence, whether they are other people, spirits, ancestors or the Supreme Being, in an effort to prevent the consequences of the offence. This African concept of sin and the need for atonement, Kunhiyop continues, "provides a bridge for presenting biblical teaching about sinful humanity and God's provision of atonement through Christ."[20] And as we know, Jesus is the perfect and final sacrificial lamb, who takes away the sins of all African peoples (John 1:29), if they look to him for salvation. He is the final, ultimate atoning sacrifice. Jesus became a penal substitutionary sacrifice for all those who would put their faith in him, and as Christ the Victor he has overcome not only sin (Rom 3:21–28; Gal 3:13; 1 Pet 2:24; 3:18; 1 John 2:1–2; 3:4–10), but also the forces of evil which are in disharmony with nature and society (Mark 3:22–27; Eph 1:20–22; 2:1–10; Heb 2:14–15; 1 Pet 3:9–22; 1 John 3:8; Rev 5:5–13).

We would do well to remember the words of the Protestant Reformer Martin Luther that we quoted in chapter 3; he understood Jesus's death on the cross as, first, an attack on sin, and second, salvation from sin. This attack on sin, he said, was a strange attack, for Jesus suffered and died at the hands of humanity. Although there might be physical consequences for sin and

---

18. Adeyemo, 283.

19. Mbiti, *Introduction to African Religion*, 117.

20. Kunhiyop, *African Christian Theology*, 70.

immorality, as Kunhiyop explains throughout his *African Christian Ethics*, the cross of Christ will in the end set African disharmony to rights (Col 1:16–20).[21] This includes reconciling humanity to each other and to God (2 Cor 5:18–20; Eph 1:15–17; Col 1:20–22). Similarly, in chapter 3 we also saw how the church father Irenaeus taught that Jesus is the second Adam, having undone the evils brought about by the first Adam, and put right every part of the disobedience of Adam and his offspring, restoring communion with God.

No doubt sin is a serious matter for Africans. But perhaps the sinful behaviour that Africans fear most is witchcraft, and not without reason. Let us dig a little deeper and explore the fearsome topic of African witchcraft, and see how it is overcome by the cross of Christ.

---

21. Kunhiyop.

11

The Cross of Christ and Witchcraft

For many Africans a belief in witchcraft is deeply ingrained in their worldview. Diseases, accidents, untimely death, inability to gain promotions at the office, failure in examinations and business, disappointments in love, barrenness in women, impotence in men, failure of crops and many other evils are said to originate from witchcraft. For Africans, witchcraft is not an illusion or a figment of the imagination, but rather forms part of the very fabric of their reality. The fear and reality of witchcraft in the daily experience of African people is oppressive! One of the greatest needs of African people is relief from this bondage. Healey and Sybertz have urged that Christianity needs to demonstrate its relevance to the people of Africa by addressing witchcraft. A person, they say, "who has gone through the experience of being bewitched and healed is able to appreciate in a deeper way what God has done for human beings in Jesus Christ."[1]

Before we continue, I must state that there are slight differences between sorcery and witchcraft, though for the most part the differences are nuanced and academic. I shall not explore these differences here; instead I refer to both simply as witchcraft.

Magic plays a significant part in African Traditional Religion. People use magic to seek to tap into and manipulate the spiritual forces for their own benefit. Almost always, magic is used to harm other people or their property. Interestingly, Awolalu understands magic as emphasizing the "omnipotence of thought." That is, he explains, "a man wishes that certain things may happen, and they do happen as he wishes – the wishes may be good or evil." Although witchcraft is intangible, it "is projected from the mind – it is psychic." Awolalu

---

1. Healey and Sybertz, *African Narrative Theology*, 218–19.

believes that humans are created powerful, able to reconstruct and demolish. When they are destructive, they act "contrary to the will of [their] Creator."[2]

Perhaps the most prominent feature of witchcraft is its antisocial nature. Kunhiyop rightly says that "witchcraft has nothing good to offer" and that "it encourages disrespect for parents and children," resulting in "disunity and hatred among families, and even murder."[3] Witches are the enemies of African society who not only harm their victims but may even kill them. This is done by casting spells from a distance, or meddling with articles of clothing, nail clippings or hair. Poison may also be used to achieve their evil intent.[4]

John Mbiti made an interesting distinction between evil spirits and witchcraft. He pointed out that insanity and psychological disturbances are usually accredited to evil spirits, even though witches might be thought responsible. Physical harm and individual illnesses are, however, accredited to witchcraft.[5] Kunhiyop makes a similar observation, saying that witchcraft "is the traditional way of explaining the ultimate cause of any evil, misfortune or death." According to him, it offers convenient explanations for events that are thought to be unnatural, such as premature death, barrenness or sterility, severe accidents, and so on.[6] On the other hand, as Khathide says, to attribute every misfortune and every mysterious accident to witchcraft undermines the opportunity for true repentance and Christian faith. He believes, and I think rightly so, that "Africans need to learn to accept responsibility for their actions and limitations."[7] Kunhiyop insists that Christians need "to understand that the ultimate source of evil is sin," and that the result of sin is death and suffering (Rom 6:23). Evil and suffering, he says, are not only a result of Adam's sin, but are also the consequences of the choices we make. For instance, if we behave promiscuously and are infected with HIV/AIDS, it is not witchcraft that we should blame, but our own immoral choices.[8]

Yet, as Kunhiyop says, missionaries and African church leaders "have dismissed belief in witchcraft as mere superstition. In doing this, they fail to understand the African worldview."[9] Having said all of the above, I, as a

2. Awolalu, *Yoruba Beliefs*, 83–84.
3. Kunhiyop, *African Christian Ethics*, 382.
4. Turaki, *African Traditional Religion*, 103.
5. Mbiti, *African Religions and Philosophy*, 44.
6. Kunhiyop, *African Christian Ethics*, 377–78.
7. Khathide, *Hidden Powers*, 350.
8. Kunhiyop, *African Christian Ethics*, 387–88.
9. Kunhiyop, 383.

Westerner, do not wish to discount belief in witchcraft, but rather to engage with it on African terms, because for Africans witchcraft is a very real threat, and it needs to be addressed appropriately and adequately.

For many Africans there is an internal rational basis for their belief in witchcraft, which has been considered by others as irrational and absurd. Those who deny the rationality of witchcraft believed in by many Africans do so on scientific grounds. However, even some rational beliefs cannot be explained in concrete terms. Think about atoms, neutrons and quantum physics, things we cannot see or feel, but we believe they exist because of mathematics or physics. Or think of a remote control for a television: most of us have no knowledge of how it works, but we know it works when we want to change channels. No doubt to some in Africa, "belief" in that remote control would be irrational.[10] Polycarp Ikuenobe tells us that a belief in witchcraft exists and is meaningful for many African people in a way that is relative to their cultural and spiritual context, which includes both their beliefs and their lived experiences. Therefore, the rationality of the belief in witchcraft should not be determined scientifically or objectively.[11]

It follows that "lived experience" provides the context in which one might believe in witchcraft. In Africa it is unhelpful to say that witchcraft is illusory, because for many Africans it is very much a part of their reality and experience, says Khathide.[12] The African belief in witchcraft should be understood relative to the African people's own perspectives, their lived experiences and their belief systems, whether we agree with it or not.[13]

Therefore, despite the fact that Africans are inclined to attribute every misfortune and accident to witchcraft, when in fact personal immoral behaviour or negligence is probably to blame, we should, I believe, give them the benefit of the doubt – without, that is, compromising a proper understanding of suffering and misfortune in light of the consequences of sin and immorality. When dealing with African culture and spirituality we should seek to understand the belief as rational on their terms.

Having examined the rationality of witchcraft, it is appropriate to explore the role of the traditional healer, sometimes called the witch doctor. Magic in the hands of these specialists is accepted by Africans as "good," and is honoured

---

10. Polycarp Ikuenobe, "Internalism and the Rationality of African Metaphysical Beliefs," *African Philosophy* 13, no. 2 (2000): 135–36.

11. Ikuenobe, "African Metaphysical Beliefs," 128.

12. Khathide, *Hidden Powers*, 342.

13. Ikuenobe, "African Metaphysical Beliefs," 130.

by society because it is believed that it treats diseases, counteracts misfortunes and wards off the evil power of witchcraft. Simply put, witch doctors are thought to be good and witches evil. Unfortunately, however, sometimes a witch doctor, who is required to have an understanding of witchcraft, takes on the persona of a witch. In such cases the functions of a witch doctor and the activities of a witch become blurred.

It is thought that traditional healers are able to tap into a mystical power and provide people with access to some of it by "infusing" it into physical objects such as rags, amulets, figures, charms, and feathers, and it may even be imparted through bodily incisions and special incantations. The objects are worn or used to protect people's compounds, fields, cattle, other property and family members from evil and witchcraft. In time, the mystical force in such paraphernalia loses its effectiveness, in which case it will need to be replenished. The idea is that the "good" magic will counteract "evil" magic, but this is true only if the "good" magic is more powerful than the enemy's magic. African Christians often experience turmoil because of their openness to this traditional healing, while feeling that one cannot be a Christian and visit a traditional specialist.

Khathide and others see a problem in the African Protestant church in that the message of God's love, the sacraments and prayers are not adequate for helping Africans handle witchcraft and the fear it presents. Catholicism, on the other hand, seems to be better at meeting this need, for it has devotional objects – for example, prayer books, the rosary, medallions and holy water. They replace the African traditional amulets and paraphernalia. Traditionally, however, Protestants have rejected such devotional objects (except perhaps prayer books in some traditional Protestant churches).[14] Khathide thinks that because of this many mainstream church members have been lost to African Initiated Churches and Pentecostal/charismatic churches, where their needs are met and they are assisted in opposing witchcraft through deliverance and exorcism.[15] Although these are important, however, I believe the problem goes much deeper! I believe that African Christians also need a theological and biblical understanding of witchcraft and the ultimate source of evil. Kunhiyop is doubtful as to whether African churches have seriously engaged with the troubling issue of witchcraft from a biblical and theological perspective. He comments, "Christian rituals are often seen as new and more powerful protection against the attacks of one's enemies and those who may

---

14. Khathide, *Hidden Powers*, 351.

15. Khathide, 351.

be jealous." It is not uncommon, Kunhiyop says, for mothers to "cover" their children's beds with the "blood of Jesus" in order to protect them from evil spirits and witchcraft. The fear of being bewitched is a growing phenomenon.[16] Khathide explains that the reality of sorcery and witchcraft in the lives of countless African Christians is apparent, and yet churches do little to take their fears seriously. In fact, discussions of witchcraft have been discouraged in churches and "interaction with other spirit beings was swept under the carpet and continued to exist away from the eyes" of clergymen and missionaries.[17]

Light maintains that the rapid growth of Pentecostalism and the African Initiated Churches is directly related to their understanding of the Holy Spirit's superior power over witchcraft. African preachers of these church movements focus less on Jesus Christ and more on the Holy Spirit and his demonstration of power.[18] The power of the Holy Spirit is vital in an African context, but, as we shall see, Jesus Christ and his atoning work is infinitely powerful as well. And I believe that emphasizing the Holy Spirit over Jesus Christ is a grievous error: the role of the Holy Spirit is to point us to Jesus.

In the context of this reality of witchcraft in the lives of African people, many are falsely accused of practising as witches. Because misfortune and death are accredited to witchcraft, some societies attempt to eliminate all witches and witchcraft. No doubt many innocent people, including children, who are thought to be witches are murdered. Jesus himself experienced similar accusations, being accused of being possessed by Beelzebul and partnering with him (Mark 3:22–27). And yet it is in fact Christ himself who conquers the evil spirits. The great novelist, medievalist and lay theologian C. S. Lewis explains this in the words of Aslan in his classic children's book *The Lion, the Witch and the Wardrobe*:

> It means . . . that though the Witch knew the Deep Magic, there is a magic deeper still which she did not know. Her knowledge goes back only to the dawn of time. But if she could have looked a little further back, into the stillness and the darkness before Time dawned, she would have read there a different incantation. She would have known that when a willing victim who had committed

---

16. Kunhiyop, *African Christian Ethics*, 383.

17. Khathide, *Hidden Powers*, 340.

18. Light, "Evangelical Church in Africa," 301–2. See also his *Transforming the Church in Africa*.

no treachery was killed in a traitor's stead, the Table would crack
and Death itself would start working backwards.[19]

Aslan the lion, in Lewis's work, is a representation of Jesus Christ. Although
this is a European literary work, Aslan's words are striking for any cultural
context, and profoundly so for the African context of witchcraft and also evil
spirits. Considering African Traditional Religion and witchcraft, Awolalu
writes, "A substitute sacrifice may be prescribed by a knowledgeable priest, to be
offered to the witches; and once the witches are satisfied with the offerings, they
will 'release' the prospective victim."[20] However, in a spectacular display, Jesus
Christ is himself the great high priest, and by his own penal substitutionary
sacrifice he offers himself up so that the "victims" of sin and Satan may be
released. Upon their release the "victims" forfeit the terrible consequences of
sin and enter into the rich blessings of God. This is precisely the imagery in C. S.
Lewis's *The Lion, the Witch and the Wardrobe*. The White Witch demanded her
right to Edmund Pevensie's execution for his act of betrayal. Aslan, however,
makes an arrangement with the witch and offers himself up in the place of
Edmund, Aslan being of much greater worth to the witch than the child
Edmund. Aslan is then slain by the White Witch on the Stone Table. After
Aslan has died, the substitutionary sacrifice made, and the departure of the
White Witch and her entourage from the stone table, Aslan victoriously rises to
life again. Although the imagery is perhaps not entirely biblical, it corresponds
clearly to the substitutionary sacrifice offered to African witches as a kind of
ransom. Jesus Christ offered himself up as a substitutionary sacrifice for us,
and although this was not offered to witches, the consequences of his atoning
sacrifice are similar to those of Aslan's sacrifice in terms of redemption. Jesus's
substitutionary death and resurrection mean that no witch or evil spirit has
a hold on any African Christian. But more than that, Jesus is also Victor and
Conqueror! The cross of Christ offers us freedom from fear of all sorts of evil,
because Christ the Victor has overcome all evil powers and they have been
made subject to him. This includes witchcraft.

African Christians have God's protection, for he has been victorious over
witchcraft. Christians need not fear, for they are promised full protection in
Christ the Victor and have been given "enough weapons to fight and defeat
witchcraft in this life."[21] Kunhiyop likewise writes that there is great comfort

---

19. C. S. Lewis, *The Lion, the Witch and the Wardrobe* (London: Geoffrey Bles, 1950), 185.
20. Awolalu, *Yoruba Beliefs*, 86.
21. Turaki, *African Traditional Religion*, 105.

in knowing that "the Christian has victory in Christ over witchcraft and all its forces" (Rev 5:5–13; 12:7–12).[22]

There is no doubt that the cross of Christ is powerful for African Christians who find themselves enslaved to the fear of witchcraft and the harm and chaos it creates. Christ alone has offered himself up as a substitutionary sacrifice, and he has overcome witchcraft and subjected it to himself through his atoning death. All the powers of witchcraft and magic in Africa aimed towards any person who is in Christ are made absolutely powerless!

---

22. Kunhiyop, *African Christian Ethics*, 389.

12

The Cross of Christ and Suffering

I often ask myself why there is so much suffering on the continent of Africa, and no doubt there are various political, social and economic reasons. I don't intend to offer reasons for suffering in this book, but I do hope to show that there is hope in the cross of Christ for the suffering experienced by countless Africans.

The question that philosophers and theologians have tried to understand for centuries is the relationship between suffering and a good God. This is called theodicy. That is, how does one explain the Judeo-Christian God's existence in view of the defects, sufferings and evil in this world? Although this sort of philosophical thinking originated in Western philosophy, these problems are also very significant for African people, especially when they experience so much evil and suffering. Most African societies believe that "God did not create what is evil, nor does he do them any evil whatsoever," according to Mbiti.[1] Evil and suffering are not just a spiritual problem, but very much a practical problem. Part of the solution to the problem of suffering, N. T. Wright believes, is understanding that God is "passionately and compassionately involved" in our world of suffering, pain and loss.[2] Yet, as Adeyemo explains, Africans generally believe that the spiritual forces and social tragedies that contribute to disharmony "are controllable and should be manipulated by them for their own purposes."[3] I shall not attempt to solve the problem of God and suffering – whoever could?! But I wish to point towards a hope in the atonement that demonstrates that Jesus has overcome the evil of suffering.

It is well known that the suffering and oppression on the continent of Africa are profound. Throughout Africa we can find examples of genocide, burned

---

1. Mbiti, *African Religions and Philosophy*, 199.
2. Wright, *Justice of God*, 40, 43.
3. Adeyemo, "Doctrine of God," 21.

villages, refugees, starvation, unemployment, overcrowding, discrimination, intimidation, violence, murder, sabotage, arson, gangsterism, poverty, hunger, devastation of war, child soldiers, HIV/AIDS, severe drought, monstrous injustices of the past, bribery and corruption, political instability, inequality, political repression, apartheid, dictatorship, warlords, gross mismanagement, abuse of power, torture, lawlessness, poor housing, low wages, inflation, homelessness (which produces discontent and worsening crime), disease (malaria, yellow fever and other deadly viruses), and so on.

Remember the serious decline in relations between the Hutu and Tutsi ethnic groups in Rwanda that led to genocide in 1994. The late environmental and political activist Wangari Maathai, a Nobel Prize winner, made mention of Sierra Leone, the Congo, Kenya, Rwanda, Uganda, Côte d'Ivoire and other African countries where there has been maiming and killing "in senseless conflicts as well as forcing vast numbers of people from their homes to live in misery in unsanitary and overcrowded encampments." She also considered the shifting rainfall patterns, which in part are "a result of global climate change" and directly threaten "the livelihoods of the majority of Africans who still rely on the land for their basic needs."[4] Although we should acknowledge a degree of human responsibility, the HIV/AIDS pandemic is also horrific in Africa. Despite all the suffering and oppression in Africa, Christianity is apparently on the rise, making it a "Christian continent." Emmanuel Katongole therefore asks the question, "Then why all the horror?"[5] N. T. Wright also asks, "How can such things happen in a world where God is supposed to be in charge?" He says that in our pain we "struggle to make sense of things that numb our senses, to find some explanation behind the inexplicable."[6]

Suffering does not always come with a clear explanation, and so many people attribute it to God in one way or another. While acknowledging apparent contradictions in Scripture, Blocher believes that God is not the author of evil or its direct cause. He views evil as in opposition to God and an absolute contrast to him.[7] Blocher, therefore, looks at evil from a different perspective from the African view. He believes that evil is "*the absence of being something*" (emphasis his); similarly, "injustice is the absence of justice," and

---

4. Wangari Maathai, *The Challenge for Africa* (London: Arrow, 2009), 10.

5. Emmanuel Katongole, *The Sacrifice of Africa: A Political Theology for Africa* (Grand Rapids: Eerdmans, 2011), 30.

6. Wright, *Surprised by Hope*, 41.

7. Henri Blocher, *Evil and the Cross: An Analytical Look at the Problem of Pain* (Grand Rapids: Kregel, 1994), 59.

so on.[8] Although God does not participate in evil, he does exercise judgement. N. T. Wright holds that the "effects of global warming and the resultant climate change" may well be "connected to human destructive greed and pollution," and could "be construed theologically as incorporating elements of God's judgement, mediated within the natural order."[9] However, Wright makes it clear that one must not affirm or assume

> that the actual people who suffer the effects of natural events like earthquakes, tsunamis, volcanoes, hurricanes, floods, and so on (whether connected or totally unconnected with human activity) are worse sinners, and therefore stand more under God's judgment, than those who are fortunate enough to live somewhere else than where the disaster struck.[10]

God's judgement, therefore, includes the often natural consequences of evil, which originates not only in evil spirits, but primarily in humanity's sinful activities. Meiring also says that "natural disasters point to tension or disharmony in the community. God is also part of this balance. An offence against another human, element of nature or ancestors, is seen as an offence to God."[11]

There seems to be a connection between our sin and the creational order. Blocher notices that all sin is "the reverse side of all creation."[12] N. T. Wright also understands that the evil activity of human beings is part of the enslavement of creation. He sees a link between evil events caused by humanity's rebellion against its Creator and "the out-of-jointness of creation itself." However, he believes that when humanity is put back to rights, so too will "the world be put back to rights."[13]

As I mentioned in the previous chapter, witchcraft is often held responsible for individual suffering, and deities and spirits in some African cultures are also understood to bring about evil and misfortune. The Supreme Being, however, is usually said to be responsible for epidemics. N. T. Wright says that "evil is the force of anti-creation, anti-life, the force which opposes and seeks to deface and destroy God's good world of space, time and matter, and above all God's

---

8. Blocher, *Evil and the Cross*, 20.
9. Wright, *Surprised by Hope*, 48.
10. Wright, 48.
11. Meiring, "As Below, So Above," 736.
12. Blocher, *Evil and the Cross*, 23.
13. Wright, *Justice of God*, 72.

image-bearing human creatures."[14] I believe that this is why death is presented by the apostle Paul as the last great enemy in 1 Corinthians 15:20–28. Indeed we can say that evil and death are defeated, because while they did their worst to Jesus on the cross, he overcame them and conquered them (1 John 3:8) by taking their full force and exhausting them, and then rising to life again after being dead for three days.

There are still contemporary issues that need to be dealt with: for one, colonialism. Bujo fittingly reminds us that colonization contributed to the ruinous economic situation that exists in Africa today, not to mention the physical suffering and slavery caused by colonization, and its mass exploitation of Africa's natural resources.[15] Nevertheless, Maathai was right to say that, in spite of the need to acknowledge colonialism as a fact in Africa's past, Africa "cannot continue to blame her failed institutions, collapsed infrastructure, unemployment, drug abuse, and refugee crises on colonialism." Africa needs to break free from its own greed and corruption, escaping its "culture of dependency that leads to passivity, fatalism, and failure." Africa must begin thinking for itself and learning from its mistakes.[16] I like what Maathai says, but it is my conviction that this can begin in a meaningful way only really once Africans come to realize the person of Jesus Christ and his atoning work – that is, his government and reign (Ps 110; Eph 1:21–23), his work of reconciliation of God and humanity and the reconciliation of human beings with one another (Eph 2:12–17; Col 1:20–22), and the forgiveness of sin (Eph 2:3–17; Col 1:22–23; 2:12–15; 1 Pet 3:24; 1 John 1:7; 2:2; 3:5).

While foreign nations brought colonization to Africa with serious consequences, Africa itself, on the other hand, is solely to blame for its ethnocentrism. Almost every war in Africa has arisen from ethnic tensions within the same country. And what is of grave concern is that many involved in these ethnic tensions and who participate in violence, murder and injustice call themselves Christians! Katongole laments that in the most Christianized African nation, Rwanda, Christians killed fellow Christians in the very places where they had worshipped together, and their churches often became killing fields. This raised serious questions about the claimed sense of the sacredness of life and community in African culture. Further, Katongole questions the status of Christianity in Africa and wonders whether it has "become so interwoven into the story of violence that it no longer had a vantage point from

---

14. Wright, 89.

15. Bujo, *African Theology*, 9.

16. Maathai, *Challenge for Africa*, 5.

which to resist the violence."[17] Kunhiyop argues that ethnocentrism makes a successful economy in Africa a near impossibility. In addition to this, economic victimization together with ethnic wars only exacerbate Africa's poverty.[18] Yet, despite such terrible circumstances, there is hope, as Kalu proclaims that the "atonement contains the promise and reality of abundant life. It is an aspiration for the poor and a message that unites people across racial, ethnic, and class boundaries."[19] It is also Katongole's hope that authentic African Christianity will "inspire the commitment of African Christians to work for a peaceful social order."[20] It is in light of this that I, too, am hopeful that African Christians will seek to live in peace with their brothers and sisters of diverse ethnic groups if they are able, among other things, to truly understand the nature of such a spectacular atonement.

A consequence of sin is, of course, suffering. Burgess notes that suffering plays a significant part in the theology of the African Pentecostal church, especially Nigerian Pentecostal theology. Often theologies of suffering have developed as Africans have reflected on their own experiences of crisis in light of Scripture and sometimes Christian tradition. A significant aspect of this theology is overcoming the enemy, usually Satan, through faith. Evil persons or evil spirits employed by Satan to work evil and misfortune "are then counteracted by means of aggressive spiritual warfare." No doubt, as Burgess explains, this demonstrates some continuity with African Traditional Religion.[21] Contrary to the African Pentecostal theology of suffering, however, Healey and Sybertz explain that the cross is a redeeming narrative which tells of a loving God who chooses to make his home among those who are victims of oppression and violence. Therefore, God does not necessarily "save human beings from suffering, but in and through suffering." It is, in fact, the broken Christ who "is the one who heals a broken world."[22] The once-broken Christ is now resurrected and alive. This is the hope that we have in Christ, a hope that in him all will be made good and well.

Here I would like to point African Christians to a promising solution, one that is not without spiritual warfare. Blocher also highlights the atonement, proclaiming that God at the cross "laid the foundation of our hope" by turning

---

17. Katongole, *Sacrifice of Africa*, 8–9.

18. Kunhiyop, *African Christian Ethics*, 150.

19. Kalu, *African Pentecostalism*, 256.

20. Katongole, *Sacrifice of Africa*, 35.

21. Burgess, "Nigerian Pentecostal Theology," 51–52.

22. Healey and Sybertz, *African Narrative Theology*, 222.

evil against itself "and brought about the practical solution to the problem. He has made atonement for sins, he has conquered death, he has triumphed over the devil." Blocher also reminds us that the evil one has been "disarmed by the expiatory blood which alone washes away sins."[23] Similarly, N. T. Wright says that the cross "has decisively addressed" the problem of evil. While Wright sees the problem of evil as a cosmological crisis, he is quick to note that the problem is also very much about us, and that God has dealt with that too on the cross.[24]

Wright views three aspects of Jesus's death which address evil. First, evil and death are confronted by Jesus on the cross and it is there that their power is exhausted and conquered. This is evident in the writings of the early church fathers, where the defeat of cosmic powers was almost primary. Second, God's forgiveness releases humanity from their guilt, but also releases himself from being angry at a world gone wrong. Third, God in the person of Jesus Christ will ultimately bring to completion the victory of the cross, whereby the final victory over the demonic forces, death and disharmony will show them to be intruders in God's world, and they will be stripped of their power (Col 2:15).[25]

Now that Jesus has won the victory through the cross and has redeemed human beings, we have the privilege of participating in God's grand narrative as his wise representatives and stewards. We are called to worship our Creator and to reflect his image in his creation, so that we might "bring his wise and healing order to the world, putting the world to rights under his just and gentle rule."[26]

Blocher also highlights Psalm 110:1, where God speaks to "my Lord," that is, Christ, commanding him to subdue his enemies. This is the first stage of the kingdom, which is one of conquest and battle. In 1 Corinthians 15:25 the apostle Paul emphasizes that Christ "must reign until he has put all his enemies under his feet," until the resurrection of his saints (1 Cor 15:20–28).[27] Wright therefore sees the Christus Victor theme as central in atonement theology, the theme on which all the other aspects find their place.[28] I differ somewhat from Wright on this. As I have said, I see penal substitution as the means of atonement and Christus Victor as its purpose. Nevertheless, Chike also considers the Christus Victor theme within the African context and says, "Africans see Jesus as the Victor because life is, as it were, a spiritual battle.

---

23. Blocher, *Evil and the Cross*, 104, 131.

24. Wright, *Justice of God*, 16, 97.

25. Wright, 136–37.

26. Wright, 139.

27. Blocher, *Evil and the Cross*, 121.

28. Wright, *Justice of God*, 114.

The African Christian is involved in many fights and so needs a warrior on his side." The fight, Chike continues, might include overcoming evil spirits, poverty or illness.[29]

The atonement, especially in light of the Christus Victor theme, offers Africans hope, since Jesus has overcome evil and suffering. Blocher tells us that God's response to evil is that he turned it back upon itself, having conquered it "by the ultimate degree of love in the fulfilment of justice." This response "consoles us and summons us. It allows us to wait for the coming of the crucified conqueror. He will wipe away the tears from every face, *soon*."[30]

Ultimately, God in Christ the Victor overcomes the evils of suffering. One day Jesus Christ will inaugurate a renewed earth and a renewed cosmos, where harmony, peace and happiness will be eternal. This inauguration, however, has its beginning now, with a new humanity.

---

29. Chike, "Proudly African, Proudly Christian," 223.
30. Blocher, *Evil and the Cross*, 133.

13

A New African Humanity

Although Africans view humanity as at the very centre of the Supreme Being's creation story, they define themselves within their relationships with one another in community as well as with the Supreme Being, the spirits and ancestors, and even with nature.[1] However, as Mbiti lamented, the traditional sense of community is being undermined and challenged, and in some ways destroyed. Emphasis, Mbiti said, "is shifting from the 'we' of traditional corporate life to the 'I' of modern individualism" as African peoples are being oriented towards individuality as a result of external influences.[2] An understanding of the cross of Christ in an African perspective may well offer hope in light of the deterioration of African community.

The French philosopher René Descartes proposed the celebrated statement *cogito, ergo sum*: "I think, therefore I am." Africans, however, understand their nature of being very differently. They say that being is ultimately wrapped up in family and community. Perhaps Dowden says it best when he writes, "Africans feel their identity grows out of family, language and culture." An African is therefore nothing without a family.[3] Playing on Descartes, Mbiti put it like this: "I am because we are, and since we are, therefore I am."[4] In this chapter I shall examine Christian identity and its role in the new African humanity established by Christ through his atonement.

Regrettably, countless Africans and their cultures have experienced dehumanization. Maathai lamented that Africans have experienced not only

---

1. Amon Eddie Kasambala, "The Impact of an African Spirituality and Cosmology on God-Images in Africa: A Challenge to Practical Theology and Pastoral Ministry," *International Journal of Practical Theology* 9 (2005): 307.

2. Mbiti, *African Religions and Philosophy*, 219.

3. Richard Dowden, *Africa: Altered States, Ordinary Miracles* (London: Portobello Books, 2009), 21, 63.

4. Mbiti, *African Religions and Philosophy*, 219.

physical colonization, but also the long-lasting effects of "colonization of the mind," a confusing of African identity. A disfigured identity is exhibited in "images of suffering and dysfunction on television, in newspapers, on websites, and in fund-raising appeals." She argued that Africans begin internalizing such images.[5] Of course, these images might be true of parts of Africa, but they are a poor and unhelpful reflection of the African people as a whole. Furthermore, African communities were told by foreigners "that their culture was demonic and primitive." Maathai believed that this contributed to a loss of Africans' sense of collective power and responsibility, and surrendered them to "commercialism, materialism, and individualism." This in turn developed into impoverishment and the loss of culture for the most part. Maathai challenged her fellow Africans to change their attitude, inspiring them to "believe in themselves again; that they are capable of clearing their own path and forging their own identity." She proclaimed that "they must rise up and walk."[6] Light similarly affirms African identity, saying that for a Christian African to deny his or her identity as an African is to be dehumanized, for God himself has placed his image in every African person, and this makes African culture possible.[7] Yet, without undermining the reality of African dehumanization, Jesus himself took on humanity in his flesh, so that he too could be dehumanized, sharing in the dehumanization of the African people (Isa 52:14; 53:2–3; Matt 12:20–21). It was in Jesus's incarnation and then his dehumanization that he achieved victory by offering himself up as an atonement for the sins of the African people, thereby conquering evil. Therefore, when he sets the world to rights, there will be no more dehumanization, for then all creation will be in harmony and without sin, and through Christ's victory dehumanization will be no more.

Maathai believed that "culture gives a people self-identity and character. It allows them to be in harmony with their physical and spiritual environment, to form the basis for their sense of self-fulfilment and personal peace." Yet Africans, she said, do not sufficiently recognize their cultural heritage.[8] However, until recently, to be a Christian in Africa was in a way to become European. Many African Christians are very thankful for the missionaries who came to Africa to preach the gospel. Unfortunately, however, many of these early missionaries robbed African Christians of their identity and African cultural heritage, with

---

5. Maathai, *Challenge for Africa*, 20, 34, 79.

6. Maathai, 20, 165, 276.

7. Light, "Evangelical Church in Africa," 286–87. See also his *Transforming the Church in Africa*.

8. Maathai, *Challenge for Africa*, 160.

lasting consequences. According to Maathai, these consequences included an inferiority complex. Their native life and culture were portrayed by European missionaries as inferior and needing to change should they wish to embrace the Christian faith.[9] Nevertheless, as Light says, the gospel of Jesus Christ does not negate culture, nor does it require deculturalization – except, he says, when the gospel is contradicted. African Christians do, however, need to be told that there is a cost to following Jesus for all Christians worldwide.[10]

All the same, there has certainly been a quest for a new African identity. Thabo Mbeki, a former post-apartheid South African president, set in motion an "African Renaissance," encouraging a restoration of a healthy African identity and black self-image following the effects of suppressive colonialism and the dehumanization experienced as a result of the apartheid regime. Adeyemo explains that Africa is searching for a new identity in several ways: "through political independence from outside rule, by recovering its own past, by playing an independent, specifically African role in world politics,"[11] and by promoting an African ecclesiastical "selfhood." Kalu has also described how "Africans have lost their own story and absorbed another people's story," namely, the story of Western people.[12] This quest for a new identity is especially evident in African Initiated Churches and African Pentecostalism. In fact, Kalu emphasizes that Africans are attracted to the spiritual aspects of the gospel which "resonate with the power theme in indigenous religions, the power that sustained the cosmos, the socioeconomic and political structures."[13]

More often than not, the quest for a new identity in the African church has led to syncretism, whereby a mixture of Christianity and African traditional beliefs coexist. African theologians have even attempted to strengthen African identity by exploring the connections between Christianity and African Traditional Religion. However, when traditional Africans convert to Christianity they often find themselves synthesizing the two religious systems for their benefit. They find it difficult to embrace Christianity wholeheartedly while also letting go of their traditional religions.

The gospel of Jesus Christ is always proclaimed within a particular cultural context – in this case, African culture; and it is not that the said culture must

---

9. Maathai, 39.

10. Light, "Evangelical Church in Africa," 274. See also his *Transforming the Church in Africa*.

11. Tokunboh Adeyemo, "A Theological Critique of Church Indigenization in Africa" (Master's thesis, Talbot School of Theology, 1976), 55, available at http://www.tren.com.

12. Kalu, *African Pentecostalism*, 4.

13. Kalu, 4.

be disregarded, but rather the gospel enriches the culture. Yes, in converting to Christianity one might expect cultural changes, but, as Ferdinando has said, Christianity does not contribute to a "loss of cultural identity"; in fact, Christianity should strengthen and reaffirm an African identity.[14] The gospel of Christ, without a doubt, offers freedom and helps Africans rediscover their dignity and cultural identity.

Although conversion to Christianity is essential for salvation, it sometimes tends to be individualistic; but it is more than that. Personal salvation is part of a universal cosmic restoration, the result of Christ's cosmic victory. Let us not forget, however, that the salvation of several individuals from the same community also makes a positive, revitalizing contribution to their community. Thus the renewal of an African humanity through salvation is both individualistic and communal. Kunhiyop believes that there is in fact individuality among African communities and that communities promote a balance between community and individual creativity.[15]

When looking towards a new Christian identity, as Bujo well says, Jesus offers Africans fullness of life, and true development. Following the pain of colonialism, the slave trade, awful refugee situations and the many other forms of suffering that Africans have faced, Jesus, the Proto-Ancestor (or the Supreme Ancestor), a new Moses, leads them through today's problems of oppression and poverty to the waters of life.[16] Dehumanization was Africa's old identity. Yet Jesus not only relates to Africans' dehumanization, but offers them a new identity, as we read in 2 Corinthians 5:15–17. African Christians have been united with Christ in his death (Rom 6:5), so that their old identity was crucified with him. This means that sin has no official hold or rights over them (Col 2:13). But if Jesus has been raised from the dead, and they are his people, being found in him, they are a new creation, for "the old has passed away; behold, the new has come" (2 Cor 5:17).

The spectacular atonement offered by Christ on the cross has affected the status of humanity as well as creation which will one day be redeemed, restored and recreated. No doubt this includes African culture and community. This means that in Christ, African humanity is being redeemed as well. Africa's oppressive past can be overcome by discovering its position within redemptive

---

14. Keith Ferdinando, "Christian Identity in the African Context: Reflections on Kwame Bediako's *Theology and Identity*," *Journal of the Evangelical Theological Society* 50, no. 1 (2007): 137.

15. Kunhiyop, *African Christian Ethics*, 23.

16. Bujo, *African Theology*, 94.

history, so that Africa can offer its own unique contribution in anticipation of an eschatological hope, a cosmic harmony and social renewal.

Both penal substitutionary atonement and the Christus Victor theme are instrumental in creating a new humanity in Christ (Eph 2:15; Rev 5:5–13). This new humanity is characterized by a new unity, a new love and a new oneness, which are qualities of peace through Jesus's atonement (Eph 2:14–15; 1 Pet 3:18). Without ignoring African culture and identity, Turaki makes it clear that "to become a member of this new humanity and community, one must leave behind all tribal gods and turn to Christ who is the Head of this new humanity and community" (Eph 1:22–23). The hatreds and divisions between African tribes and people groups have now been abolished by Christ's atoning work on the cross for those Africans who are in Christ (Eph 2:12–19; Col 1:20–21). Turaki therefore thinks that "a new humanity has been created in Christ which has the capacity to love, forgive, fellowship, commune, worship and to live at peace with itself and with others."[17] Despite the terrible, oppressive predicaments in which African people have often found themselves, the African identity can be fully expressed in Jesus through his atoning work. Ultimately, such a Christian identity will find expression in a new African humanity, forming a harmonious African community.

As we have mentioned, family and community are central to Africa's social system and are a significant aspect of their economic, political and cultural life. In chapter 5 we mentioned the term *ubuntu*, which Light explains as that which "captures the community spirit in African communities: it stresses the values of respect, human dignity and compassion."[18] Turaki says that "the church of Jesus Christ is the new community of believers founded upon the redemptive work of Christ on the cross. It is a new humanity redeemed and recreated in Christ Jesus."[19] The church should then live Jesus's message and mission within its own cultural background.

For any of us – though especially for an African – to be truly human is to belong to community. This involves participating in the ceremonies, rituals, festivals and beliefs of the community. Africans who isolate themselves from the religion and culture of their group sever their roots, for their communities in some way make them aware of their existence. As we have seen, Christianity challenges African Traditional Religion, but if understood properly it seems also

---

17. Turaki, *Uniqueness of Jesus Christ*, 43, 45, 53.

18. Light, "Evangelical Church in Africa," 115. See also his *Transforming the Church in Africa*.

19. Turaki, *Uniqueness of Jesus Christ*, 89.

to engage with African thought and culture positively. Furthermore, as Turaki has said, the community gives purpose and meaning to life for traditional Africans, and is both the judge and the lawgiver. And so it is believed that there is "no life, no hope, no peace, no identity, no destiny and no existence, in short no salvation" outside of the community.[20] Kasambala explains that to hold to African spirituality means to understand the harmonization of interpersonal relationships.[21] That is, as Turaki explains, "the community is held together holistically, spiritually, dynamically and communally in a network that defines their relationships, roles and functions."[22] Such a sense of community stretches beyond a local community into a universal community of beings and the so-called "non-beings" whose relationships reveal a harmonious cosmic order.

For Africans, as we have seen, the consequences of sin are always communal. Sin is said to bring evil or misfortune to the community. The relationships of human beings or the breakdown thereof affects the works of spirits as well. It is thought that even the breakdown of a relationship between a living human and an ancestor is an offence against the Supreme Being. The living and the "living dead" are still in community, and the Supreme Being is also understood to be a member of that community. These relationships are interconnected. Such an offence is likely, it is believed, to bring about tension, disasters and disharmony. Sin in an African community, therefore, requires cleansing, a penalty, an atonement – typically by the shedding of the blood of an animal. Such a sacrifice cleanses both the offenders as well as the community and protects them from the consequences of the sin.[23] Although sin clings closely to us and we are to lay it aside by abandoning it, Jesus takes sin upon himself and deals with it, offering atonement by enduring the cross (Rom 3:24–26; Gal 3:15; 1 John 1:1–2; 3:5). Jesus becomes not only the founder but also the perfecter of our faith (Heb 12:2). For African Christians, then, and their communities, Christ has dealt with their sin and its relation to the spiritual world, and thus no further cleansing, penalty or atonement is required. However, this does not mean that an offender should not be held responsible for his or her sin or disobedience of moral values. Naturally, these cause "misfortune"; for example, sexual diseases might result from adultery and promiscuity, and imprisonment for theft or murder, and so on.

---

20. Turaki, 118.
21. Kasambala, "African Spirituality and Cosmology," 305.
22. Turaki, *Uniqueness of Jesus Christ*, 58.
23. Nyeri, "Gong Traditional Religion."

Chike observes that, as we have noted above, an African person is defined by his or her relationships in a community. An idea of who that person is in him- or herself is almost absent from a traditional African culture. Rather, it is the person's function within the community that is important. Logically, this applies to African thinking about Christ as well. For Africans, the question is not so much who Jesus is, but rather who he is *to Africans*. Africans are therefore not so much concerned with who Jesus is, in and of himself, but rather with what he does. It is for this reason that they easily accept Jesus as the Provider, Healer and Victor.[24] Therefore, an understanding of Christ is tightly tied to an understanding of salvation. An African Christian understanding of salvation usually places emphasis on the social and communal aspects of salvation, says Kwabena Asamoah-Gyadu. "The restoration of the community is also present in the Christian understanding of salvation as a process of reconciliation with God."[25] It is through Jesus Christ the Victor that God reconciles humanity and the world to himself.

Turaki explains that the reconciliation of humankind in Christ on the cross is foundational for permanent peace and harmony in community and in the world. It is only in Jesus Christ, he says, "that we have the basis of destroying human selfishness and greed as well as the enmity between all human beings in their tribes, races, nations and classes."[26] I must make it clear that it is only through sacrifice that there can be harmony and forgiveness between humans and their communities, their ancestors, the spiritual world and God, and Jesus Christ has made that sacrifice once and for all! This reconciliation and oneness is the effect of Christ's new creation. Humanity is being recreated in him, as part of a renewed creation (2 Cor 5:17). As we have seen, this hope is firmly rooted in the cross of Christ.

African life consists of integrated parts making up a whole which "is governed by a law of harmony." The objective is to preserve a state of peace. Ideally, "the traditional African seeks to live in harmony and to balance his life in a harmonious and peaceful existence with his entire world and especially with the spirit world," says Yusufu Turaki.[27] It is only by a divine reconciliation that the "image of God" in humanity is renewed. Humankind enjoys restoration with God and in community (Eph 2:17–19). This reconciliation is reason for great celebration! Among African peoples, where there has been reconciliation

---

24. Chike, "Proudly African, Proudly Christian," 234.

25. Asamoah-Gyadu, "African Cosmology, Community, and Christianity," 60.

26. Turaki, *Uniqueness of Jesus Christ*, 44.

27. Turaki, 33.

with other peoples or communities, a celebration is usually in order, where meals and drinks are shared signifying peace and harmony with each other. In Matthew 26:26–29, the celebration of the Lord's Supper is precisely this: a celebration of reconciliation between people and God, and with one another. The imagery of the blood being poured out in verse 28 presents Jesus as the self-giving sacrifice, and reminds us not only of the Old Testament temple sacrifices and rituals, but also of those of African Traditional Religion. This is the blood of a *new* covenant, a new order of harmony and reconciliation, where the sins of many have been forgiven by God and Christ, the Supreme Ancestor. And so, by his penal substitutionary death, Jesus cancels the guilt and punishment of sin. Although the Lord's Supper replaces the Hebrew Passover celebration, it is the ultimate reconciliation celebration for the African people, anticipating harmony in a new community, a new humanity and a renewed creation. This newness is already set in motion, and every time Africans celebrate the Lord's Supper, they identify with this newness and reconciliation now and in the future as they experience Christ's presence among them in an extraordinary way.

The gospel is sufficient in meeting people's needs and letting them live as an example of Jesus in resisting Satan and preaching the gospel. Katongole says, "God's dream is the dream of a new generation, a new family, a new community, and a new 'tribe' beyond Hutu, Tutsi, and Twa" (John 10:16–18; 12:32). In a stunning expression of what Christ has done in the lives of some children of Maison Shalom, a children's home in Burundi, Katongole records how when they were asked by a journalist whether they were Hutu or Tutsi, they replied, "No, we are Hutsitwacongozungu,"[28] a nickname that combines various ethnical identities. Sometimes children get it before adults do! These children affirmed the very reality of a new humanity which has been created in Christ and which transcends old human divisions. Those who are "born again" into the Christian faith, in Christ Jesus, are born into a "new humanity and new creation." As Turaki says, "a new humanity, a new community of believers, is now being formed."[29] This is evident in 2 Corinthians 5:15–17, on the foundation that Jesus died for humanity and was raised to life.

When Africans, along with the rest of humanity, are redeemed, they become "genuine human beings in a fuller sense than they otherwise would have been." Further, genuine human beings, from Adam and Eve onwards, are given the command and responsibility to care for creation and to bring order

---

28. Katongole, *Sacrifice of Africa*, 180–81.
29. Turaki, *Uniqueness of Jesus Christ*, 42.

to God's world by creating and maintaining communities.[30] Although they are not simply maintaining it, as N. T. Wright says, but bringing it to a state of peace and harmony. This is the intent of the cross of Christ!

The very heart of Africans is for African communities to enjoy harmony, which begins now in the present, and is ultimately realized in a renewed creation. The Christian community, with Christ as its head, is founded upon his redemptive work on the cross. Therefore, African identity and African community find their richness and completeness in Christ and his atonement. We will next look at the significance of the atonement for the end of the age: cosmic harmony and an African hope.

---

30. Wright, *Surprised by Hope*, 199.

14

Cosmic Harmony and an African Hope

Cosmic harmony is really the climax of the African hope. In this chapter I will describe how the African hope is intrinsically this-worldly and physical, and fulfils the very yearnings of the African people as told in their myths and legends.

African people generally have a different concept of time from the Western world. Traditionally, Africans do not perceive time linearly, which explains why they are able to understand the events of Jesus's ministry as if they were in the present, even though they occurred long ago. Gehman tells us that Westerners understand time in terms of abstraction regulated by a clock, and programme events in keeping with a calendar. Africans, on the other hand, conceive of time in terms of the concrete, as experienced in events. Africans are event-oriented, rather than time-oriented. This means that "time is measured by participation in an event" and is experienced as cyclical.[1]

Furthermore, as I have explained, reality for Africans is divided into the physical world and the world of spirits. At death, says Kalu, the life or soul of the person lives on, continuing in "a new lifecycle in the spirit world," becoming an ancestor.[2] Death is thought to be not the end, but the beginning of a new stage of life. The cyclical view of time means that there is a continuation of life even after death.

The African theologian John Mbiti said that for Africans, "the future is virtually absent because events which lie in it have not taken place," and therefore they do not organize time. However, he continued, if "future events

---

1. Richard J. Gehman, *African Traditional Religion in Biblical Perspective*, rev. ed. (Kampala: East African Educational Publishers, 2005), 60.

2. Kalu, *African Pentecostalism*, 176.

are certain to occur, or if they fall within the inevitable rhythm of nature, they at best constitute only *potential time*." Africans set their minds on the events that have already taken place, rather than on future events.[3] Yet Mbiti claimed that the African concept of time is uninterested in life "beyond a few months from now"; the future is therefore "virtually non-existent as *actual* time, apart from the relatively short projection of the present up to two years."[4] Neither is there in African thought a concept of history moving towards an ultimate end in the future, ushering in a "golden age," according to Mbiti. This means that there is no concept of a "messianic hope" or a final judgement.[5]

John Mbiti's understanding, however, has not gone without challenge. Byang Kato, also an African theologian, identified several major problems, two of which are, first, that Mbiti made African people think and reason as one people, despite diverse ethnicities, beliefs and cultures. And second, "the African who cannot conceive the future is yet able to plan the marriage of an unborn baby!" – and, of course, the planning of ceremonies for the rite of passage when the child is still very young is also problematic.[6]

In a private interview with African Ernest Balintuma Kalibala, who was a Harvard PhD graduate in anthropology, Kato recorded that he "strongly rejected the notion that Africans cannot conceive of the future." Kalibala felt that "the African theologian who believes that kind of thing is following what Europeans have taught him. He has not been home to find out things for himself."[7] When Kato himself conducted a survey among five hundred or so African college students, he found that about 90 percent had placed their faith in Christ as a result of hearing a message about his second coming in the future.[8] Bujo also criticized Mbiti, saying that Africans do indeed cherish the traditions of their ancestors, not for the sake of the past, but for the sake of the present and the future. In fact, Bujo is convinced that "the present-day African is thinking eschatologically, of those last times when all will be changed."[9]

Although there is little apparent relation between Africans' concept of time and atonement theology, an understanding of it is helpful for the rest of this chapter. African people generally *do* think eschatologically about the end

---

3. Mbiti, *African Religions and Philosophy*, 17.

4. Mbiti, 21.

5. Mbiti, 23.

6. Kato, "Incipient Universalism," 91–92.

7. Kato, 94.

8. Kato, 117.

9. Bujo, *African Theology*, 31.

of the age, and therefore a future cosmic harmony and an African hope are not entirely foreign.

This brings us to the spiritual nature of ancestors. According to African philosophy, one's life does not move in a straight line, but like the African concept of time, life is somewhat circular. Other than the fact that some people become ancestors, Africans are not entirely sure what happens to people once they die, but they do believe that people continue to exist for ever after death in one way or another. African Traditional Religion does not comment further than this. Most traditional Africans also do not believe in a judgement in a life after death.

However, Bujo says that dying Africans have a sense of participating in the life-force of their ancestors, and that there is no sign "of despair in the face of death, and no sense that one is being deprived of life."[10] Ancestors are dependent upon the recognition of their descendants for their continued authority. They become lost once they are forgotten, and their authority as superiors to their offspring is then diminished.[11] Similarly, Mbiti explained that when an ancestor is no longer remembered personally by name by those who are still alive, the process of death is made complete. Yet it is thought that the ancestors do not vanish from existence, but rather join the community of spirits, thus entering a "collective immortality."[12] This, of course, is very different from the Christian concept of resurrection (see 1 Cor 15:20–28). Jesus's atoning work and his resurrection offer us life eternal, a physical resurrection! Nevertheless, Africans also share some sense of resurrection and eschatology that is not too dissimilar from that of the Christian faith.

At the start, an important distinction needs to be made. Although I draw on African tradition, the remainder of this chapter focuses on the implications of the cross of Christ for African Christians who should believe in the resurrection. In the very beginning, before the fall of humanity, human beings possessed immortality. Mbiti recorded stories of creation from several African societies, writing, "Man was originally put in a state of happiness, childlike ignorance, immortality or ability to rise again after dying. God also provided him with the necessities of life, either directly or through equipping him to develop them, and man lived more or less in a state of paradise."[13] In another work Mbiti wrote that many African myths described how human

---

10. Bujo, 124.

11. Nürnberger, *Christ and the Ancestors*, 25.

12. Mbiti, *African Religions and Philosophy*, 26.

13. Mbiti, 93.

beings were meant to live for ever. In these myths, apparently, God gave one or more of three gifts: the first one was immortality, the second, "the gift of becoming young again after getting old," and the third, resurrection – that is, if a person died he or she would be raised to life once again.[14]

Mbiti also provided the following examples. In a Bambuti myth, it is said that God provided the first people with shelter, food, immortality and the gift of rejuvenation when people got old. In those days they lacked nothing and lived happily. The Tswana say that the primordial human beings lived in a state of peace and blessedness; they "neither ate, nor drank, nor died." The Bushmen say that humanity lost the gift of resurrection and began dying. Lastly, the Chagga share the same view as the Bushmen, but explain that a connection "between heaven and earth was broken, the bliss of the 'heavenly country' also disappeared, and men must die in order to return to the other world."[15]

Regrettably, the order was disrupted and resulted in tragic consequences for humanity. Before this turn of events, people lived in a golden age, and yet many "have lost even the mythological sight of it," said Mbiti. Except perhaps for ancestral beliefs, Mbiti lamented that to his knowledge "there is not a single myth" which seeks "to suggest a solution or reversal of this great loss." Nevertheless, as Mbiti wrote, behind these myths is a glimpse that there lie "the tantalizing and unattained gift of the resurrection, the loss of human immortality and the monster of death."[16]

Mbiti explained that ancestors, while remembered by the living, still maintain their personalities, sexual distinctions, and political and social statuses. In fact, although their spirits are separated from their bodies, their "human activities are reproduced in the hereafter, the wealth or poverty of the individual remains unchanged, and in many ways the hereafter is a carbon copy of the present life." That is, the "physical-social characteristics of [the ancestors'] human life" still remain very much intact.[17] However, as I have already said, when the last person who knew the person who is now an ancestor "dies, the living-dead is removed from the state of personal immortality." The ancestor then sinks into oblivion and joins the community of spirits. Here the ancestor loses his or her personal name and personality and becomes an "it." Therefore,

---

14. Mbiti, *Introduction to African Religion*, 85.
15. Mbiti, *African Religions and Philosophy*, 93, 96.
16. Mbiti, 93, 96.
17. Mbiti, 157.

as Mbiti continues, human beings are "destined to lose [their] humanness but gain [their] full spiritness."[18]

Christianity has traditionally presented a concept of heaven which is similar in some ways to ancestral belief. The word "heaven" to indicate the ultimate end of the redeemed was popularized by the medieval church and later piety, but fails to do justice to the Christian hope. So, contrary to the modern view of heaven, N. T. Wright, the great New Testament scholar, explains that the early Christians rarely spoke about heaven, but when they did so "they seemed to regard this heavenly life as a temporary stage on the way to the eventual resurrection of the body." Paradise or heaven is believed to be the "blissful garden" where the people of God rest prior to bodily resurrection.[19] Therefore, the ultimate hope of a Christian is not so much about "'going to heaven when you die,' but being bodily raised into the transformed, glorious likeness of Jesus Christ."[20] Although the word "heaven" might be an appropriate word to express rest after death, the idea is somewhat vague. But this is a prelude to something very different, something that also emphatically involves earth – a renewed earth. For this is where Jesus's reign will take place (see Ps 110). This is precisely why the New Testament "regularly speaks not of our going to be where Jesus is but of his coming to where we are," says N. T. Wright.[21] Christopher Wright, another theologian (don't get confused between N. T. Wright and Christopher Wright), also believes that "those who die in Christ enjoy a state of rest, waiting for the return of Christ to earth, the resurrection of the body, and the final judgement." Wright argues that Revelation 21–22 says nothing about going to heaven, but that God will come to earth and will transform the whole of creation in a new heaven and a new earth, and that he will dwell among us. With no small amount of humour, Wright wrote, "Even as a young Christian it struck me as an unhealthy attitude to life and the world. . . . This world is my home. God put me here on earth for a purpose and I want to live here for him. The angels can go beckon someone else. I'm staying."[22]

Maathai rightly argued that "as Christianity became embedded in Africa, so did the idea that it was the afterlife that was the proper focus of a devotee, rather than this one – a legacy that continues to affect development." She

---

18. Mbiti, 157–58.

19. Wright, *Surprised by Hope*, 41.

20. Wright, 168.

21. Wright, 190.

22. Christopher J. H. Wright, *The God I Don't Understand: Reflections on Tough Questions on Faith* (Grand Rapids: Zondervan, 2008), 194.

lamented, "Putting so much emphasis on the delights of heaven and making it the ultimate destination devalues life in the present." If all delight is to be found in heaven and not on earth, then this surely encourages people to remain passive.[23] She was right; but she also missed the proper understanding of the resurrection and the renewed earth which we read about in Scripture, and which changes everything!

Traditional Africans do not have an eschatological hope of bodily resurrection, at least not in such a dramatic sense as presented in the Holy Scriptures (see 1 Cor 15:12). Yet, in a well-known African myth, a chameleon "is featured as the messenger who should have brought news of immortality or resurrection, but either lingered on the way, or altered the message slightly or stammered in delivering it."[24] So the idea of resurrection is not altogether foreign to African thought, even if it is conceived as something in the past rather than in the new world to come. It is also thought that an "initiate comes to new life by a kind of death and resurrection and reaches fullness of personhood."[25]

Unlike the African concept of salvation and resurrection, the biblical concept of salvation emphasizes resurrection as an event in salvation when cosmic harmony will eventually be established. N. T. Wright explains that salvation for the Christian in its fullest sense is not merely about souls (like disembodied ancestors), but the whole human being. This salvation is as much about the present as it is about the future, and it is about what God "does *through* us, not merely what God does *in and for* us" (emphasis original).[26] God longed "to re-establish his wise sovereignty over the whole creation, which would mean a great act of healing and rescue." A major purpose of salvation, Wright believes, is to "rescue humans *in order that humans might be his rescuing stewards over creation*" (emphasis original; Col 1:12–14).[27] This is what the kingdom of God is all about!

Resurrection and the renewed earth offer an ultimate hope for African Christians. The Christus Victor theme points us towards the purpose of Jesus's atoning work, the resurrection, "the annihilation of the power of death" (see John 12:31–32; 1 Cor 15:26). Resurrection life, according to Moltmann, "is not a further life after death," but "it means the annihilation of death in the victory

23. Maathai, *Challenge for Africa*, 40.
24. Mbiti, *African Religions and Philosophy*, 51.
25. Bujo, *African Theology*, 85.
26. Wright, *Surprised by Hope*, 200.
27. Wright, 202.

of the new, eternal life" (1 Cor 15:55).[28] Moltmann views the cross of Christ as God identifying with humanity's suffering. Accordingly he writes, "Easter was a prelude to, and a real anticipation of, God's qualitatively new future and the new creation in the midst of the history of the world's suffering."[29] Christ's resurrection as well as ours ought to be expressed "materially as the realm of the power of the resurrection in a world which has fallen a prey to death, and thus to the other cosmic powers" (1 Cor 5:20–28), says Moltmann.[30] There is no belief in redemption in African Traditional Religion in terms of future resurrection; it is therefore at this point that resurrection highlights the importance and centrality of Jesus, who is Victor over Death. Jesus, having risen from the dead, is greater than death, for he has overcome it (John 10:15–18).

In African Traditional Religion, death is in the end unnatural, usually being attributed to evil spirits, witchcraft and misfortune. Death should never happen. Even though death may result in an ancestral status, it ultimately leads to total loss of personality and identity. Once the ancestral spirit sinks into oblivion, African Traditional Religion offers no hope! But Christ has conquered the evil spirits, witchcraft and death, and therefore, through the cross of Christ, Jesus offers a salvation which begins in this life and stretches forward throughout eternity, finding expression in a perfect humanity.

Resurrection for the Christian anticipates "ultimate salvation, the healing transformation of space, time, and matter." From the time of Jesus's resurrection and his victory over death, this "future rescue" that was promised to us had already begun.[31] Considering the meaning of the atonement, N. T. Wright raised the following questions, which I have adapted: "How can I participate in the resurrection and the renewed creation despite my sin and the punishment I deserve?" The answer ought to be, "Because Jesus has borne *my* penalty and has made good by offering himself as a substitutionary atonement" (Isa 53; John 1:29; Rom 3:21–26; Col 2:13–14; 1 Pet 2:23–24; 3:18; 1 John 2:2). And if the question is asked, "How can God's plan to rescue and renew the entire world go ahead despite the corruption and decay that have come about because of human rebellion?," the answer ought to be, "Because on the cross and through the atonement, Jesus defeated the powers of evil and death, which have enslaved rebel humans and so ensured continuing corruption"[32] (John

---

28. Moltmann, *Crucified God*, 170.
29. Moltmann, 163.
30. Moltmann, 180.
31. Wright, *Surprised by Hope*, 199.
32. Wright, 199.

12:31–32; Eph 1:20–23; Heb 2:14–15; 1 Pet 1:18–19; 1 John 3:8; Rev 5: 5–10; 12:7–12). Similarly, Weaver sees salvation as freedom from the evil forces, and in our freedom we are shaped and changed by God's reign to participate in making the reign of God visible throughout history.[33] Atonement, I believe, is really the "engine" behind the resurrection. Or worded differently, penal substitution is the means of atonement, and Christus Victor is its purpose (Col 1:12–14; 2:12–15; 3:18–22).

Referencing Romans 8, N. T. Wright highlights Paul's use of the exodus imagery in relation to the whole of creation. Accordingly, creation is at present in slavery, like the children of Israel in Egypt – or in African philosophical terms, in disharmony. Yet God's desire was and is to rule creation through his image-bearing people. This was a promise for the future, that someday a true human being, the image of God himself, God's incarnate Son, "would come to lead the human race into their true identity."[34]

In traditional African myths throughout the continent, it is told that heaven and earth were once very close, or joined together, and that God was close to humankind. In fact, Adeyemo says that in these oral traditions, heaven was so close to earth that one could stretch out one's hand and touch it, and there were no limitations in communicating between the two. This "was a happy relationship between God and man."[35] Sadly, these myths also describe the severing of that relationship between heaven and earth as a result of human sin and disobedience.

Africa's harmonious balance includes abundant life in terms of "good health, fruitfulness, economic abundance, the power of procreation," and of course cosmic harmony, which is at the very centre of African existence.[36] For Africans, a balance of harmony "must be maintained between God and man, the spirits and man, the departed and the living." Suffering and misfortune result when this balance is upset, and as I have demonstrated, the African continent (and in fact the whole world) experiences a multitude of sufferings. It seems obvious to me that Africa for the most part is in a state of continual disharmony and imbalance!

A proper understanding of salvation and the African Christian hope ought to bring a harmonious balance, that is, cosmic harmony and recreation. Turaki

---

33. J. Denny Weaver, *The Nonviolent Atonement*, 2nd ed. (Grand Rapids: Eerdmans, 2011), 46.

34. Wright, *Surprised by Hope*, 103.

35. Adeyemo, "Concept of Salvation," 53, 55.

36. Asamoah-Gyadu, "African Cosmology, Community, and Christianity," 54.

said that it was at the cross that the "final consummation of our salvation and restoration of the new created order took effect" (Rom 8:18–25; Rev 20–21). Cosmic harmony and balance find their meaning and fulfilment "in Christ's work of reconciliation, re-creation and regeneration of both the fallen humanity and the fallen creation"[37] (2 Cor 5:17–19; Eph 2:12–22; Col 1:20–22; 2:12–14; Rev 5:9–10). N. T. Wright believes that Christians are designed "to be a sign and foretaste of what God wants to do for the entire cosmos." More than this, they are "*part of the means by which* God makes this happen in both the present and the future" (emphasis his). Through the "stewardship" of these "redeemed humans . . . creation will at last be brought back into that wise order for which it was made" (Rom 8:18–2).[38]

Christopher Wright takes this a step further than N. T. Wright. He considers Revelation 21:24–27 and says that the "honour of the nations" (v. 26) is the increase "of cultural achievement over many generations. Art, literature, music, architecture, styles of food and dress, the richness of language and culture – and so much else – these are the things that national distinctives are built on."[39] No doubt the African people will have much to participate in and to contribute to this renewed creation, with all its diverse ethnicities, cultures and languages.

The renewed creation starts "with the unimaginable reservoir of all that human civilization has accomplished in the old creation – but purged, cleansed, disinfected, sanctified, and blessed," says Wright. He continues, "It is the redeemed, resurrected humanity who will have the eternal joy of building upon such a reservoir, in such brilliant creativity. In their resurrected glory, humanity will finally fulfil their creation mandate."[40]

Without such a spectacular atonement, there is no victory over sin, evil and death, and therefore no resurrection! It is only through the cross of Christ that Africans can at this moment not only look forward to renewal and cosmic harmony, but even now, as those who are redeemed, have the privilege of participating in such a grand cosmic project. In fact, the whole biblical narrative is all about God getting his people to participate in restoring his creation. As we read in Anselm's *Cur Deus Homo*, sin and disobedience upset the ordered relationship of beauty and harmony, the consequence being disharmony and disorder. Jesus Christ the God-man, however, offered himself up to death as a sacrifice, which was not required, but was freely given to satisfy God's honour

---

37. Turaki, *Uniqueness of Jesus Christ*, 46.
38. Wright, *Surprised by Hope*, 200.
39. Wright, *The God I Don't Understand*, 201.
40. Wright, 202, 210.

and his anger towards humanity's disobedience. And one day Africa and the world will be restored, and peace and harmony will be enjoyed for ever.

N. T. Wright says that Jesus proclaimed God's kingdom not as a heavenly reality, but as "something that was happening in and on this earth, through his work, then through his death and resurrection, and then through the Spirit-led work" in which many would be called to participate.[41] The cross of Christ, together with Jesus's resurrection, was not designed to take us away from earth, but instead to make us a means of the transformation of Africa, and of this whole world, anticipating Africa's coming renewal and cosmic harmony. Even the church father Irenaeus of Lyons wrote of how the fallen Adam was resumed by Christ, who inaugurated a new humankind, a new creation, a new cosmos, which would find its fulfilment in Jesus. This new world will enjoy the elimination of death, the removal of sin and evil, and the enjoyment of resurrected bodies. Africa will once again enjoy the lost gifts of immortality and resurrection spoken about in their legends, and God himself will dwell among us as King establishing peace on earth for ever.

---

41. Wright, *Surprised by Hope*, 203.

Bibliography

Abelard, Peter. *The Letters of Héloïse and Abelard*. Harmondsworth: Penguin, 1974.

Achebe, Chinua. *Things Fall Apart*. 50th Anniversary ed. New York: Anchor, 1994.

Adeyemo, Tokunboh. "African Traditional Concept of Salvation in the Light of Biblical Teaching." Master's thesis. Talbot School of Theology, 1976. Available at http://www.tren.com.

———. "The Doctrine of God in African Traditional Religion." PhD diss. Dallas Theological Seminary, 1978. Available at www.tren.com.

———. "A Theological Critique of Church Indigenization in Africa." Master's thesis. Talbot School of Theology, 1976. Available at http://www.tren.com.

Adeyemo, Tokunboh, General ed. *Africa Bible Commentary*. Nairobi: WordAlive, 2006.

Allison, Gregg R. *Historical Theology: An Introduction to Christian Doctrine*. Grand Rapids: Zondervan, 2011.

Anselm. *Proslogium; Monologium; An Appendix in Behalf of the Fool by Gaunilon; and Cur Deus Homo*. 1099. Translated by Sidney Norton Deane. Chicago: Open Court Publishing, 1926. Christian Classics Ethereal Library. Accessed 1 May 2011. http://www.ccel.org/ccel/anselm/basic_works.html.

Aquinas, Thomas. *Summa Theologica*. Translated by the Fathers of the English Dominican Province. New York: Benziger Bros., 1947.

Asamoah-Gyadu, J. Kwabena. "'The Evil You Have Done Can Ruin the Whole Clan': African Cosmology, Community, and Christianity in Achebe's *Things Fall Apart*." *Studies in World Christianity* 16, no. 1 (2010): 46–62.

Athanasius, *On the Incarnation*. In Series 2, vol. 4 of *The Nicene and Post-Nicene Fathers*. Edited by Philip Schaff and Henry Wace. 14 vols. Reprint. Grand Rapids: Eerdmans, 1975.

———. *Orations against the Arians*. In Series 2, vol. 4 of *The Nicene and Post-Nicene Fathers*. Edited by Philip Schaff and Henry Wace. 14 vols. Reprint. Grand Rapids: Eerdmans, 1975.

———. *In Illud Omnia: on Luke 10:22 (Matthew 11:27)*. In Series 2, vol. 4 of *The Nicene and Post-Nicene Fathers*. Edited by Philip Schaff and Henry Wace. 14 vols. Reprint. Grand Rapids: Eerdmans, 1978.

Aubert, Annette Gundrum. "Luther, Melanchthon, and Chemnitz: The Doctrine of the Atonement with Special Reference to Gustaf Aulén's Christus Victor." Master's thesis, Westminster Theological Seminary, 2002. Available at www.tren.com.

Augustine, *On the Holy Trinity*, Series. 1, vol. 3 of *The Nicene and Post-Nicene Fathers*. Edited by Philip Schaff and Henry Wace. 14 vols. Reprint. Grand Rapids, MI: Eerdmans, 1975.

———. *Acts Or Disputation Against Fortunatus The Manichaean,* 14:4, Series 1, vol. 4 of *The Nicene and Post-Nicene Fathers.* Edited by Philip Schaff and Henry Wace. 14 vols. Reprint. Grand Rapids: Eerdmans, 1975.

Aulén, Gustaf. *Christus Victor: An Historical Study of the Three Main Types of the Idea of Atonement.* 1931. Translated by A. G. Herbert. Eugene: Wipf & Stock, 2003.

Awolalu, J. Omosade. "Sin and Its Removal in African Traditional Religion." *Journal of the American Academy of Religion* 44, no. 2 (1976): 275–87.

———. *Yoruba Beliefs and Sacrificial Rites.* New York: Athelia Henrietta Press, 1996.

Barth, Karl. *The Doctrine of God, Part 1.* Volume 2 of *Church Dogmatics.* Translated by G. W. Bromiley. Edited by G. W. Bromiley and T. F. Torrance. Edinburgh: T&T Clark, 1957.

———. *The Doctrine of Reconciliation, Part 1.* Volume 4 of *Church Dogmatics.* Translated by G. W. Bromiley. Edited by G. W. Bromiley and T. F. Torrance. London: T&T Clark, 1956.

Bediako, Kwame. *Christianity in Africa: The Renewal of a Non-Western Religion.* Edinburgh: Edinburgh University Press, 1995.

———. *Jesus and the Gospel in Africa: History and Experience.* New York: Orbis, 2004.

Berkhof, Louis. *Systematic Theology.* Grand Rapids: Eerdmans, 1996.

Berkouwer, G. C. *Studies in Dogmatics: The Work of Christ.* Grand Rapids: Eerdmans, 1965.

Blocher, Henri. *Evil and the Cross: An Analytical Look at the Problem of Pain.* Grand Rapids: Kregel, 1994.

Bock, Darrell L. *Luke 1:1 – 9:50.* Baker Exegetical Commentary on the New Testament. Grand Rapids: Baker Academic, 1994.

Boersma, Hans. *Violence, Hospitality and the Cross: Reappropriating the Atonement Tradition.* Grand Rapids: Baker Academic, 2004.

Boyd, Gregory A. *God at War: The Bible and Spiritual Warfare.* Downers Grove: InterVarsity Press, 1997.

———. "The 'Christus Victor' View of the Atonement." Online blog, 2018, accessed 14 October 2022, http://www.gregboyd.org/essays/essays-jesus/the-christus-victor-view-of-the-atonement/.

Bruce, F. F. *The Epistle to the Hebrews.* The New International Commentary on the New Testament. Rev. ed. Grand Rapids: Eerdmans, 1990. Logos library system.

Brunner, Emil. *The Mediator: A Study of the Central Doctrine of the Christian Faith.* Philadelphia: Westminster Press, 1968.

Bujo, Bénézet. *African Theology in Its Social Context.* Translated by J. O'Donohue. Eugene: Wipf & Stock, 1992.

Burgess, Richard. "Freedom from the Past and Faith for the Future: Nigerian Pentecostal Theology in Global Perspective." *PentecoStudies* 7, no. 2 (2008): 29–63.

Calvin J. *Institutes of the Christian Religion.* Trans. by H. Beveridge. Peabody: Hendrickson Publishers, 2008.

Carson, D. A. *Collected Writings on Scripture.* Compiled by Andrew David Naselli. Wheaton: Crossway, 2010.

———. *Matthew.* Volume 8 of *The Expositor's Bible Commentary.* General editor F. E. Gaebelein. Grand Rapids: Zondervan, 1984.

———. *Scandalous: The Cross and the Resurrection of Jesus.* Wheaton: Crossway, 2010.

Chalke, Steve, and Alan Mann. *The Lost Message of Jesus.* Grand Rapids: Zondervan, 2003.

Chike, Chigor. "Proudly African, Proudly Christian: The Roots of Christologies in the African Worldview." *Black Theology: An International Journal* 6, no. 2 (2008): 221–40.

Clark, Jawanza Eric. "Reconceiving the Doctrine of Jesus as Savior in Terms of the African Understanding of an Ancestor: A Model for the Black Church." *Black Theology: An International Journal* 8, no. 2 (2010): 140–59.

Denney, James. *Studies in Theology: Lectures Delivered in Chicago Theological Seminary.* Third edition. London: Hodder & Stoughton, 1895.

Dowden, Richard. *Africa: Altered States, Ordinary Miracles.* London: Portobello Books, 2009.

Edwards, Jonathan. "History of Redemption." In volume 2 of *The Works of Jonathan Edwards.* 1773. Peabody: Hendrickson, 1993.

———. "Sinners in the Hands of an Angry God." 8 July 1741. Christian Classics Ethereal Library. Accessed 1 June 2014. https://www.ccel.org/ccel/edwards/sermons.sinners.html.

Ferdinando, Keith. "Christian Identity in the African Context: Reflections on Kwame Bediako's *Theology and Identity.*" *Journal of the Evangelical Theological Society* 50, no. 1 (2007): 121–43.

Ferguson, Sinclair B. "Christus Victor et Propitiator: The Death of Christ, Substitute and Conqueror." In *For the Fame of God's Name: Essays in Honor of John Piper,* edited by S. Storms and J. Taylor, 171–89. Wheaton: Crossway, 2010.

Forde, Gerhard O. *On Being a Theologian of the Cross: Reflections on Luther's Heidelberg Disputation, 1518.* Grand Rapids: Eerdmans, 1997.

Gehman, Richard J. *African Traditional Religion in Biblical Perspective.* Revised edition. Kampala: East African Educational Publishers, 2005.

Green, Joel B., and Mark D. Baker. *Recovering the Scandal of the Cross: Atonement in New Testament and Contemporary Contexts.* Wheaton: IVP Academic, 2000.

Harper, Brad. "Christus Victor, Postmodernism, and the Shaping of Atonement Theology." Paper presented at the Evangelical Theological Society, 53rd National Conference, Colorado Springs, CO, 14–16 November 2001. Accessed 2 July 2011. http://www.tren.com.

Healey, Joseph, and Donald Sybertz. *Towards an African Narrative Theology.* New York: Orbis, 2004.

Heim, Mark S. *Saved from Sacrifice: A Theology of the Cross.* Grand Rapids: Eerdmans, 2006.

Hengel, Martin. *The Atonement: The Origins of the Doctrine in the New Testament*. Translated by J. Bowden. Eugene: Wipf & Stock, 1981.

Hilary of Poitiers, *Homily on Psalm 53*, Series 2, vol. 9 of *The Nicene and Post-Nicene Fathers*. Edited by Philip Schaff and Henry Wace. 14 vols. Reprint. Grand Rapids: Eerdmans, 1975.

Hoekema, Anthony A. *Saved from Grace*. Grand Rapids: Eerdmans, 1989.

Idowu, Bolasi E. *Olódùmarè: God in Yoruba Belief*. London: Longmans, 1962.

Ignatius. "Epistle to the Smyrneans." In *The Apostolic Fathers with Justin Martyr and Irenaeus*. Volume 1 of *The Ante-Nicene Fathers*. Edited by A. Roberts and J. Donaldson. New York: Cosimo Classics, 2007.

Ikuenobe, Polycarp. "Internalism and the Rationality of African Metaphysical Beliefs." *African Philosophy* 13, no. 2 (2000): 125–42.

Jeffery, Steve, Michael Ovey, and Andrew Sach. *Pierced for Our Transgressions: Rediscovery of Penal Substitution*. Nottingham: Inter-Varsity Press, 2007.

Kalu, Ogbu. *African Pentecostalism: An Introduction*. Oxford: Oxford University Press, 2008.

Kasambala, Amon Eddie. "The Impact of an African Spirituality and Cosmology on God-Images in Africa: A Challenge to Practical Theology and Pastoral Ministry." *International Journal of Practical Theology* 9 (2005): 300–23.

Kato, Byang. "A Critique of Incipient Universalism in Tropical Africa." PhD diss., Dallas Theological Seminary, 1974.

Katongole, Emmanuel. *The Sacrifice of Africa: A Political Theology for Africa*. Grand Rapids: Eerdmans, 2011.

Kelly, J. N. D. *Early Christian Doctrines*. Fourth edition. London: Adam & Charles Black, 1968.

Khathide, Agrippa Goodman. *Hidden Powers: Spirits in the First-Century Jewish World, Luke–Acts and in the African Context*. Second edition. Johannesburg: Acad SA, 2007.

Kunhiyop, Samuel Waje. *African Christian Ethics*. Nairobi: HippoBooks, 2008.

Lewis, C. S. *The Lion, the Witch and the Wardrobe*. London: Geoffrey Bles, 1950.

Light, Vernon E. "The Evangelical Church in Africa: Towards a Model for Christian Discipleship." Extended Master's thesis, Fort Hare University, 2010.

———. *Transforming the Church in Africa: A New Contextually-Relevant Discipleship Model*. Bloomington: AuthorHouse, 2012.

Lloyd-Jones, Martyn. *God the Father, God the Son*. Volume 1 of *Great Doctrines of the Bible*. Wheaton: Crossway, 2003.

———. *Romans: An Exposition of Chapters 3.20 – 4.25 – Atonement and Justification*. Edinburgh: The Banner of Truth Trust, 1970.

Luther, Martin. *Commentary on Galatians*. Logos edition. Dallas: Word Incorporated, 1996.

———. *The Large Catechism*. Translated by F. Bente and W. H. T. Dau. St. Louis: Concordia, 1921.

————. *Luther's Works*. Edited by J. Pelikan and H. T. Lehmann. Philadelphia: Fortress, 1955–1974.

Maathai, Wangari. *The Challenge for Africa*. London: Arrow, 2009.

Mann, Alan. *Atonement for a "Sinless" Society: Engaging with an Emerging Culture*. Milton Keynes: Paternoster, 2005.

Martyr, Justin. "Dialogue with Trypho the Jew." In *The Apostolic Fathers with Justin Martyr and Irenaeus*. Volume 1 of *The Ante-Nicene Fathers*. Edited by A. Roberts and J. Donaldson. New York: Cosimo Classics, 2007.

Mbiti, John S. *African Religions and Philosophy*. Second edition. Oxford: Heinemann Educational, 1989.

————. *Concepts of God in Africa*. New York: Praeger, 1970.

————. *Introduction to African Religion*. Second revised edition. Oxford: Heinemann Educational, 1991.

McDonald, H. D. *The Atonement of the Death of Christ: In Faith, Revelation, and History*. Grand Rapids: Baker, 1985.

McKnight, Scot. *A Community Called Atonement*. Nashville: Abingdon, 2007.

————. *Jesus and His Death: Historiography, the Historical Jesus and Atonement Theory*. Waco: Baylor University Press, 2005.

Meiring, Arno. "As Below, So Above: A Perspective on African Theology." *HTS Teologiese Studies/Theological Studies* 63, no. 2 (2007), 733–50.

Moltmann, Jürgen. *The Crucified God: The Cross of Christ as the Foundation and Criticism of Christian Theology*. Minneapolis: Fortress, 1993.

Murray, John. *Redemption: Accomplished and Applied*. Edinburgh: The Banner of Truth Trust, 1955.

Ngong, David Tonghou. "Salvation and Materialism in African Theology." *Studies in World Christianity* 15, no. 1 (2009): 1–21.

Nkansah-Obrembong, James. "The Contemporary Theological Situation in Africa: An Overview." *Evangelical Review of Theology* 31, no. 2 (2007): 140–50.

————. "Sin in African Perspective." In *Global Dictionary of Theology: A Resource for the Worldwide Church*, edited by W. A. Dyrness and V. Kärkkäinen, 825–26. Downers Grove: InterVarsity Press, 2008.

Nürnberger, Klaus. *The Living Dead and the Living God: Christ and the Ancestors in a Changing Africa*. Pietermaritzburg: Cluster Publications, 2007.

Nyende, Peter. "Hebrews' Christology and Its Contemporary Apprehension in Africa." *Neotestamentica* 41, no. 2 (2007): 361–81.

————. "Why Bother with Hebrews? An African Perspective." *The Heythrop Journal* 46, no. 4 (2005): 512–24.

Nyeri, M. "A Biblical and Theological Study of the Concept, Meaning and Practice of Atonement in Gong Traditional Religion." Master's thesis. Jos ECWA Theological Seminary, 2011.

Oden, Thomas C. *How Africa Shaped the Christian Mind: Rediscovering the African Seedbed of Western Christianity*. Downers Grove: InterVarsity Press, 2007.

146   Spectacular Atonement

Orobator, Agbonkhianmeghe E. *Theology Brewed in an African Pot*. New York: Orbis, 2008.

Oswalt, John N. *The Book of Isaiah Chapters 40–66*. The New International Commentary on the Old Testament. Grand Rapids: Eerdmans, 1998.

Owen, John. *The Death of Death in the Death of Christ*. Edinburgh: The Banner of Truth Trust, 1959.

Packer, J. I., and Mark Dever. *In My Place Condemned He Stood: Celebrating the Glory of Atonement*. Wheaton: Crossway, 2007.

Parrinder, Geoffrey. *African Traditional Religion*. Westport: Greenwood Press, 1976.

Reed, Rodney, and Gift Mtukwa. "Christ Our Ancestor: African Christology and the Danger of Contextualization." *Wesleyan Theological Journal* 45, no. 1 (2010): 144–63.

Reeves, Michael. "Introducing Anselm." Online lecture, 2011. Accessed 22 February 2011 at http://www.theologynetwork.org/historical-theology/getting-stuck-in/introducing----anselm-of-canterbury.htm.

Sawyerr, Harry. *God: Ancestor or Creator? Aspects of Traditional Belief in Ghana, Nigeria and Sierra Leone*. London: Longman, 1970.

Shaw, Ian J., and Brian H. Edwards. *The Divine Substitute: The Atonement in the Bible and History*. Leominster: Day One Publications, 2006.

Siekawitch, Larry. "The Evolution of the Doctrine of the Atonement in the Medieval Church: Anselm, Abelard and Aquinas." *McMaster Journal of Theology and Ministry* 9 (2007–2008): 3–30.

Spurgeon, Charles H. "Sorrow at the Cross Turned into Joy." Sermon no. 1442, 3 November 1878. Spurgeon Gems. Accessed 4 June 2011. https://www.spurgeongems.org/sermon/chs1442.pdf.

Stott, John R. W. *The Cross of Christ*. Nottingham: Inter-Varsity Press, 1989.

———. *The Letters of John: An Introduction and Commentary*. Tyndale New Testament Commentary 19. Revised edition. Grand Rapids: Eerdmans, 1988. Logos library system.

Tidball, Derek, David Hilborn, and Justin Thacker, eds. *The Atonement Debate: Papers from the London Symposium on the Theology of Atonement*. Grand Rapids: Zondervan, 2008.

Turaki, Yusufu. *Foundations of African Traditional Religion and Worldview*. Nairobi: WordAlive, 2006.

———. *The Uniqueness of Jesus Christ*. Nairobi: WordAlive, 2006.

Turretin, Francis. "The Necessity of the Atonement." Chapter 1 of *The Atonement of Christ*. Translated by J. R. Wilson. A Puritan's Mind. Accessed 2 May 2011. https://www.apuritansmind.com/puritan-favorites/francis-turretin/the-necessity-of-the-atonement/.

Ukah, Asonzeh Franklin-Kennedy. "The Redeemed Christian Church of God (RCCG), Nigeria. Local Identities and Global Processes in African Pentecostalism." PhD diss., Kulturwissenschaftliche Fakultät der Universität Bayreuth, 2003.

Warfield, B. B. *The Person and Work of Christ*. Edited by S. G. Craig. Philadelphia: Presbyterian & Reformed, 1950.

———. *The Saviour of the World*. Edinburgh: The Banner of Truth Trust, 1916.

Weaver, J. Denny. *The Nonviolent Atonement*. Second edition. Grand Rapids: Eerdmans, 2011.

Wiredu, Kwasi. "Death and the Afterlife in African Culture." In *Person and Community: Ghanaian Philosophical Studies 1*, edited by K. Gyekye and K. Wiredu. Washington: Council for Research in Values and Philosophy (1992), 137–52.

Wright, Christopher J. H. *The God I Don't Understand: Reflections on Tough Questions on Faith*. Grand Rapids: Zondervan, 2008.

Wright, N. T. "The Cross and the Caricatures: A Response to Robert Jenson, Jeffrey John, and a New Volume Entitled *Pierced for Our Transgressions*." Fulcrum, Eastertide 2007. Accessed 18 June 2010. https://www.fulcrum-anglican.org.uk/articles/the-cross-and-the-caricatures/.

———. *Evil and the Justice of God*. Downers Grove: InterVarsity Press, 2006.

———. *Surprised by Hope: Rethinking Heaven, the Resurrection, and the Mission of the Church*. New York: HarperOne, 2008.

Langham
PARTNERSHIP

Langham Literature and its imprints are a ministry of Langham Partnership.

Langham Partnership is a global fellowship working in pursuit of the vision God entrusted to its founder John Stott –

> *to facilitate the growth of the church in maturity and Christ-likeness through raising the standards of biblical preaching and teaching.*

Our vision is to see churches in the Majority World equipped for mission and growing to maturity in Christ through the ministry of pastors and leaders who believe, teach and live by the word of God.

Our mission is to strengthen the ministry of the word of God through:
- nurturing national movements for biblical preaching
- fostering the creation and distribution of evangelical literature
- enhancing evangelical theological education

especially in countries where churches are under-resourced.

Our ministry

Langham Preaching partners with national leaders to nurture indigenous biblical preaching movements for pastors and lay preachers all around the world. With the support of a team of trainers from many countries, a multi-level programme of seminars provides practical training, and is followed by a programme for training local facilitators. Local preachers' groups and national and regional networks ensure continuity and ongoing development, seeking to build vigorous movements committed to Bible exposition.

Langham Literature provides Majority World preachers, scholars and seminary libraries with evangelical books and electronic resources through publishing and distribution, grants and discounts. The programme also fosters the creation of indigenous evangelical books in many languages, through writer's grants, strengthening local evangelical publishing houses, and investment in major regional literature projects, such as one volume Bible commentaries like *The Africa Bible Commentary* and *The South Asia Bible Commentary.*

Langham Scholars provides financial support for evangelical doctoral students from the Majority World so that, when they return home, they may train pastors and other Christian leaders with sound, biblical and theological teaching. This programme equips those who equip others. Langham Scholars also works in partnership with Majority World seminaries in strengthening evangelical theological education. A growing number of Langham Scholars study in high quality doctoral programmes in the Majority World itself. As well as teaching the next generation of pastors, graduated Langham Scholars exercise significant influence through their writing and leadership.

To learn more about Langham Partnership and the work we do visit **langham.org**

www.ingramcontent.com/pod-product-compliance
Lightning Source LLC
Chambersburg PA
CBHW072013090426
42740CB00011B/2174